The Wellness Guide

Creating A Healthy Lifestyle

Anelys Perez

THE WELLNESS GUIDE

THE WELLNESS GUIDE

THE WELLNESS GUIDE

This book is intended for informational and educational purposes only. The information provided is not intended to replace professional medical, psychological, or health advice. Readers should consult qualified healthcare professionals regarding any medical or mental health concerns or before making changes to their health routines.

The author and publisher disclaim responsibility for any adverse effects resulting from the use or application of the information contained in this book.

Names, characters, businesses, organizations, places, events, and incidents described in this book are either the product of the author's imagination or used in a fictitious manner. Any resemblance to actual people, living or dead, or actual events is purely coincidental.

First Edition

Email : ap.mindfulliving@gmail.com

Website : www.apmindfulliving.com

Dedication

I dedicate this book to my beautiful daughter. You are my everything.

I extend my deepest gratitude to my wonderful parents, my loving husband, and my amazing family. Your love and support mean more to me than words can express.

Finally, I dedicate this book to you, the reader, a seeker of joy and well-being, striving to live a life filled with happiness, balance, and good health.

THE WELLNESS GUIDE

Table of Contents

THE WELLNESS GUIDE

Introduction

Congratulations on taking the courageous first step toward wellness! This journey begins with a commitment to renewing your life and enhancing your mental and physical health. Every significant change starts with a decision, and you have made that decision. As you read this book, you will learn to cultivate joy and inner peace, prioritizing self-care as one of the most valuable gifts you can give yourself.

Many people feel physically and mentally exhausted, overwhelmed, or struggling to find time for themselves while navigating life's challenges. This book will guide you in transforming these feelings into a more balanced existence. It is important to recognize that while certain situations may be beyond your control, you can change how you perceive and respond to them.

Human beings have fundamental needs, such as sleep, nutrition, exercise, relaxation, and mental well-being. Fulfilling these needs will empower you and make you able to deal with life's difficulties and keep you stable to enjoy your daily life. Stress and tension do not come from situations but from your interpretation of them, which can be influenced by your mental and physical state.

This guide offers practical activities to help you mentally detox from negative thoughts and cultivate a positive outlook. Imagine waking up each morning with a heart full of hope, ready to embrace the world. As the first light filters through your window, you feel a sense of renewal, a fresh start that invites you to greet the day with optimism. You know you have responsibilities to fulfill as well as activities that bring you joy, keeping your mind focused and fueling your desire to start the day.

The stress and tension that once seemed ever-present now feel lighter, and even the most routine tasks hold meaning—a warm cup of tea, the sound of birds outside, or the gentle breeze that greets you as you step outside. By putting the knowledge you gain here into practice, you can transform daily challenges into opportunities for resilience and fully savor the simple moments of joy.

Mental health professionals, including myself, have utilized the techniques discussed here to assist others in enhancing their lives. If you are in therapy, consider this book a valuable supplement, offering insights and practices to strengthen your resilience during challenging discussions with your therapist.

This book explores five key elements contributing to your overall well-being: sleep quality, nutrition, exercise, relaxation, and mental health. Each chapter guides you in integrating these components into a wellness routine you can adapt at your own pace. By embracing the simple act of self-care, you will find inspiration to continue making positive choices, allowing you to replenish your mental and physical health despite your many responsibilities.

With research-based insights and actionable strategies, this book will help you reveal your full potential and achieve a fulfilling life. Whether you aim to enhance your relationships, improve your professional performance, or cultivate balance, you will discover clarity, purpose, and self-awareness as you progress on this transformative journey.

Important Note

Remember that attaining wellness is a gradual process. The activities presented in the upcoming chapters may initially seem overwhelming, but you do not have to tackle them all at once. The goal is to help you understand their benefits and encourage you to start small. Begin with one activity from a chapter and gradually build upon it. If committing to a new habit feels challenging, start with something simple and manageable, then progress to the next steps at your own pace.

For instance, you might focus on improving your sleep quality for the next month. Once you have established better sleep habits using the strategies outlined in the sleep chapter, you can move on to the nutrition chapter. It is about finding what works best for you and adapting the information to fit your circumstances.

While motivation can spark the beginning of a new habit, discipline is equally essential. Discipline will keep you moving forward even when motivation wanes, or obstacles arise. It is the foundation for maintaining consistency and staying committed to your wellness journey.

Remember, this guide is flexible. You do not have to follow every aspect of the routine or apply all the recommendations strictly. The aim is to incorporate elements that contribute to your overall well-being in a way that suits your life.

May this journey bring you fulfillment as you take each step toward a healthier, more balanced life.

The Author

5

Habits

Habits

As you explore this wellness guide, you will find new activities and suggestions in each chapter designed to help improve your well-being. Before diving into the upcoming chapters, it is essential to understand how to implement these new practices and gradually turn some of them into lasting habits.

Habits often form through repeated actions over time, becoming so ingrained that we perform them without thinking. This process does not happen overnight; habits develop through consistent repetition and intentional effort (Stojanovic, Fries, & Grund, 2021).

Recent research highlights the crucial role of self-efficacy, your belief in your ability to achieve specific tasks, in building habits. Studies show that when you feel confident about performing a habit, this self-assurance strengthens the habit over time and reduces potential distractions that could disrupt the process (Stojanovic, Fries, & Grund, 2021). These insights underscore how a strong sense of self-efficacy can enhance habit formation and sustain motivation.

When reflecting on your habits, you might notice how they shape your self-view, especially when it comes to "bad" habits. It is easy to label yourself as "lazy" if you regularly stay up late and only get five hours of sleep, resulting in low energy and spending your day on the couch scrolling through your phone. However, this is not necessarily laziness; it could be the result of sleep deprivation.

If you struggle to concentrate on important tasks, consider the factors affecting you. Do you get good-quality sleep? Do you eat nutritious foods? Are you taking any medications that may have side effects like decreased focus? Consult your doctor about recommendations if necessary. By examining your habits and identifying areas for improvement, you can avoid adopting a negative narrative about yourself and work toward a healthier lifestyle.

Creating realistic habits requires careful planning. After choosing a habit to develop, write down your motivation for it and keep this reminder handy when you find it hard to stay on track. If you anticipate potential obstacles, list them along with strategies to overcome them. For example, imagine you want to eat more fruit but may not have time to shop frequently. You can overcome this obstacle by utilizing various strategies that fit your lifestyle. Consider ordering groceries online to save time or buying fruits in bulk and freezing them for later use. Incorporating fruit into your weekly meal prep can also make healthy snacking more accessible.

Currently, your daily routine consists of many automatic actions that might not contribute to the healthy lifestyle you want. Establishing new habits is a powerful way to improve your daily effectiveness. Automating simple actions allows you to focus more time and energy on other goals. With this guide, you can identify which new habits to incorporate into your life to enhance your well-being.

Below is a template to help you track and develop healthy habits discussed in this book. As you practice each habit, assess how automatic it feels over time. If after 30 days you still need reminders, keep working on it or pair it with an existing habit. For instance, if you want to consume more fruit, you can add fruit slices to your water or make a morning smoothie with breakfast. Use visual cues like Post-it notes or phone alarms as reminders.

Habits are a fundamental part of your wellness journey because transforming your life means embracing new, healthier actions.

Takeaway

Start Small and Build Gradually: Habits take time to form; focus on small, manageable actions that you can repeat daily.

Believe in Your Ability: Trust in your capacity to build new habits—this confidence (self-efficacy) is crucial for making behaviors automatic.

Anticipate and Plan for Obstacles: Identify potential barriers to your new habit and plan solutions in advance, like scheduling time for grocery shopping if your habit involves eating more fruit.

Make Habits Visible: To reinforce your new habits, place reminders in your environment, such as putting fruit on the counter.

Leverage Existing Habits: Pair your new habit with an established one (e.g., drinking infused water with meals) to increase the likelihood of success.

Track Your Progress: Regularly check in on how automatic your habit feels. If it's not automatic after 30 days, keep working on it and adjust your approach if needed.

Remember the Long-Term Benefits: Adopting healthy habits enables you to direct your attention toward meaningful goals and enhances your overall quality of life.

New Habit

Habit (simple, clear, and realistic)
Motivation (what is driving you to acquire this new habit?)
Plan (steps to achieve the goal)
Adjust (what adjustments might you need to make if you encounter challenges/obstacles?)
Track (how will you track your progress and measure the success of your habit?)

Believe You Can Do It!

Chapter 1
The Secrets of Good Quality Sleep

Chapter One

The Secrets of Good Quality Sleep

The first element in this wellness guide is the importance of quality sleep. Sleep plays a vital role in our overall well-being, yet many people struggle to get enough rest due to work demands, personal responsibilities, and other factors. While some believe they can adapt to less hours of sleep, experts from the American Academy of Sleep Medicine advise that adults should get at least seven hours of sleep each night for optimal performance during the day (Get Enough Sleep, 2022).

The timing, duration, and quality of your sleep are interconnected with your quality of life (QoL) (Kudrnáčová & Kudrnáč, 2023). Making sleep a priority can have significant benefits, as highlighted by the National Heart, Lung, and Blood Institute. A good night's sleep not only helps prevent heart disease and other serious health issues like diabetes but also reduces stress, enhances mood, and boosts concentration (National Heart, Lung, and Blood Institute, 2022). By recognizing the importance of quality sleep and taking steps to improve your sleep patterns, you can enhance your overall well-being and lead a more fulfilling life.

If you are not sure whether your sleep routine is conducive to a healthy rest, here are some questions to help you assess it:

1. Do you go to bed with a full stomach?

2. Do you engage in late-night exercise, close to your bedtime?

3. Do work or other responsibilities occupy your mind before sleep?

4. Do you typically sleep less than seven hours each night?

If you answered "yes" to most of these questions, you might want to keep reading to discover ways to enhance the quality of your sleep. It's common to experience difficulties falling or staying asleep, especially during times of life changes or heightened stress. Before we delve into effective tips and solutions for better sleep, let's explore the processes that occur during sleep and the factors influencing the ability to fall asleep.

Circadian Rhythm

Chronobiology is a branch of biology that explores natural physiological rhythms in living organisms and how they synchronize with solar and lunar cycles. Within this field, circadian rhythms are described as inherent behavioral, physical, and mental changes that follow a 24-hour cycle in response to light and darkness (Choi et al., 2020). As part of the circadian rhythm, your eyes play a vital role in processing light, communicating to the brain whether it's daytime or nighttime, thus influencing your sleep-wake cycle. Two crucial hormones involved in this rhythm are melatonin, produced by the brain when darkness sets in, and cortisol, released by the brain upon waking in the morning to initiate an alert state.

Melatonin, known for its role in facilitating sleep at night, can be negatively affected if you expose yourself to blue light from electronic devices late at night. Such exposure disrupts the natural suppression of melatonin, making it harder for you to fall asleep as your brain receives light when it shouldn't. Conversely, exposure to sunlight in the morning aids in regulating melatonin and cortisol levels throughout the day. The impact of morning sunlight goes beyond your sleep-wake cycle. As an essential aspect of your wellness routine, ensuring sufficient exposure to sunlight during the day can significantly contribute to the quality of your sleep at night (Choi et al., 2020). Thus, prioritizing morning sunlight becomes a valuable strategy to enhance your overall sleep patterns and well-being.

For example, imagine a person who struggles with occasional sleep disturbances, finding it challenging to fall asleep at night and waking up feeling tired and groggy. They decide to implement a simple change in their daily routine – taking a walk outside and soaking up the morning sunlight. Over time, they notice a significant improvement in their sleep quality and overall sense of well-being, feeling more rested and energized during the day. This transformation is attributed to the positive influence of sunlight on their circadian rhythm and hormonal balance, proving the value of integrating sunlight exposure into their wellness routine.

What Happens In Your Sleep?

As you fall asleep, your body may relax, and your eyes close, but your brain remains actively engaged, performing essential functions while you rest. So, what happens when you are sleeping? During sleep, your brain undergoes distinct stages, known as Non-REM and REM (Rapid Eye Movement) sleep, cycling through various states throughout the night. (National Heart Lung and Blood Institute, 2011).

Stage 1 of Non-REM Sleep marks the initial phase of slumber, characterized by light sleep that allows easy awakening, while your body's muscles begin to relax. This stage typically lasts for several minutes after you fall asleep (National Heart Lung and Blood Institute, 2011).

During Stage 2 of Non-REM Sleep, your slumber remains light, but now your heartbeat and breathing gradually slow down, and your body temperature decreases. Brain wave activity also slows down with occasional bursts of electrical activity. Throughout the night, your brain cycles through this stage more frequently than others (National Heart Lung and Blood Institute, 2011).

Stage 3 of Non-REM Sleep is a deep and restorative phase that takes up a substantial part of the first half of the night, essential for feeling well-rested in the morning. During this stage, your muscles are fully relaxed, and both your heartbeat and breathing rate decrease to their lowest levels. The body releases important hormones and undergoes tissue growth and repair. Brain waves are slow, and it becomes considerably difficult to awaken you during this stage (National Heart Lung and Blood Institute, 2011).

Following these Non-REM stages, REM Sleep takes center stage approximately 90 minutes after you fall asleep. During REM Sleep, your breathing may become fast and irregular, and your closed eyes move rapidly from side to side. Additionally, your heart rate and blood pressure increase, while the muscles in your arms and legs experience temporary paralysis to prevent you from acting out your dreams. Although dreaming can occur during Non-REM sleep as well, the most vivid and memorable dreams take place during REM Sleep (National Heart Lung and Blood Institute, 2011).

Note: In addition to getting at least seven hours of sleep, it is important to move through these stages of sleep without frequent interruptions in order to feel well rested and function optimally during the day. To better understand how these stages unfold during the night, consider the example of someone who follows a well-balanced daily routine.

Throughout the day, this person prioritizes healthy habits that support good sleep. They spend time in morning sunlight, practice gratitude, devote time to relaxation, complete their work responsibilities, engage in regular exercise, stay adequately hydrated, and consume nutritious meals.

As evening approaches, the body naturally begins preparing for sleep. Melatonin levels gradually increase, signaling that it is time to rest. Understanding the importance of good sleep hygiene, the person chooses to go to bed around 10:30 pm and avoids stimulating activities such as watching television or using a cellphone before bedtime.

When sleep begins, the body first enters Stage 1 of Non-REM sleep, the lightest stage of sleep, where the heart rate begins to slow and the body starts to relax. After a few minutes, the brain transitions into Stage 2 of Non-REM sleep, during which the heart rate and body temperature continue to decrease.

After approximately twenty to thirty minutes, the body enters Stage 3 of Non-REM sleep, the deepest and most restorative stage. During this phase, the body carries out important processes such as tissue repair, hormone release, and physical recovery. It becomes much more difficult to awaken someone during this stage.

Approximately ninety minutes after falling asleep, the body enters REM sleep, the stage most commonly associated with vivid dreaming. During this phase, breathing may become faster and more irregular, and the eyes move rapidly beneath the eyelids. At the same time, the body temporarily relaxes most muscles to prevent physical movement during dreams.

Throughout the night, the brain cycles through these stages multiple times, allowing the body and mind to benefit from each phase of sleep. When a person is able to sleep continuously through these cycles, they are more likely to wake up feeling refreshed and restored.

For example, someone who goes to bed around 10:30 pm and wakes up at approximately 6:30 am may complete several full sleep cycles, obtaining the recommended seven to eight hours of sleep. Upon waking, exposure to morning sunlight helps increase cortisol levels while melatonin levels decrease, allowing the body to feel alert and ready to begin the day.

However, if sleep is frequently interrupted by external noise, notifications from electronic devices, or late-night screen use, the deeper stages of sleep may be disrupted. As a result, a person may wake up feeling tired rather than energized.

Similarly, staying up late watching television or using electronic devices can shorten total sleep time, preventing the body from obtaining the restorative sleep it needs. Over time, insufficient sleep can negatively affect productivity, mood, and daily decision-making. Fatigue may lead someone to rely on caffeine for energy, skip exercise, or choose less nutritious foods instead of preparing balanced meals.

Maintaining a consistent sleep schedule and practicing good sleep hygiene supports the natural progression through the sleep stages and allows the body to fully benefit from restorative sleep. Developing these healthy habits can significantly improve overall well-being, energy levels, and daily functioning.

Benefits of Sleep

In a comprehensive study examining the relationship between sleep and verbal memory consolidation, researchers investigated patients with REM sleep behavior disorder (RBD) (dream-enacting behaviors like talking, yelling, sitting, punching, kicking, etc.). The participants completed two verbal memory tasks in the evening, which were followed by nocturnal video-polysomnography and morning recall assessments to evaluate night-time consolidation. Additionally, a subset of nine RBD patients underwent daytime consolidation assessments to explore morning learning/recall and evening recall (cross-over order). Notably, two RBD patients with dementia were studied separately (Uguccioni et al., 2013).

The findings revealed that patients with RBD, including those with dementia, experienced sleep-related consolidation for verbal memory. Despite the disruptive behaviors exhibited during REM sleep, their ability to retain and remember verbal information was not compromised (Uguccioni et al., 2013). This discovery sheds light on the critical role of sleep-in memory consolidation, emphasizing the significance of a consistent and healthy sleep routine for promoting optimal cognitive functioning and memory in the general population.

Sleep provides essential rest for your cardiovascular system, allowing your heart rate and blood pressure to gradually slow during non-REM sleep as you enter deeper stages. Additionally, during REM sleep, heart and breathing rates can fluctuate in response to dreams, which seems to promote cardiovascular health. Furthermore, while asleep, your body generates more cytokines, vital cellular hormones that support the immune system in combatting infections. Ensuring sufficient sleep is crucial for increasing your body's ability to defend against common infections (National Heart Lung and Blood Institute, 2011).

Sleep also has a role in regulating appetite, energy utilization, and weight management. While asleep, the body experiences increased production of the appetite suppressant leptin and decreased levels of the appetite stimulant ghrelin. Inadequate sleep is associated with a higher likelihood of being overweight or obese and a preference for consuming calorie-rich and carbohydrate-heavy foods (National Heart Lung and Blood Institute, 2011). This underscores the interconnectedness of sleep with the other key elements covered in this wellness guide, such as nutrition, exercise, relaxation, and mental well-being, and how it contributes to their overall positive impact on your life.

Sleep Disorders and Disturbances

When it comes to sleep, these are factors that disrupt your sleep during the night preventing you from sleeping the necessary number of hours or interrupting the stages of sleep previously discussed in the chapter. The most prevalent sleep disorders include sleep apnea, insomnia, narcolepsy, and restless legs (National Heart Lung and Blood Institute, 2011). If you suspect you might be experiencing any of these sleep disorders, it is advisable to consult your doctor.

Some experts may recommend a sleep study to identify the specific sleep disorder you might be presenting. This study involves monitoring your oxygen levels, breathing, heart rate, and brain waves. Using the data collected during the study, they can determine the appropriate treatment to help you achieve effective sleep across all sleep stages.

Additionally, there are other examples of common factors that can disrupt your sleep, such as caffeine, nicotine, and medications containing steroids and decongestants. In the case of caffeine, this substance is believed to suppress the cell receptors that adenosine, a substance in the brain, uses to initiate its sleep-inducing signals.

This leads the body to perceive itself as not tired. The effects of caffeine can last for as long as six to eight hours before completely wearing off. As a result, consuming a cup of coffee in the late afternoon may affect your ability to fall asleep at night. Furthermore, anxiety disorders, bipolar disorder, schizophrenia, and depression can also contribute to sleep disturbances (National Heart Lung and Blood Institute, 2011).

Sleep Hygiene Action Plan

A restful night's sleep is not solely determined by your bedtime habits; rather, it is influenced by your daily activities and lifestyle choices. Many experts and researchers have proposed the following sleep hygiene tips (sleep habits) because they can help you optimize your sleep and wake up refreshed (National Heart Lung and Blood Institute, 2011):

1. **Morning Sun**: Take in the morning sun (but consult your doctor if you have a health issue).

2. **Consistent Schedule**: Train your brain with a set bedtime and wake-up time, even on weekends.

3. **Embrace the ZZZs**: Aim for 7 to 8 hours of uninterrupted sleep each night.

4. **Listen to Your Body**: Go to sleep when you feel sleepy. Don't force it.

5. **Escape the Sleepless Cycle**: If sleep doesn't come within 20 minutes, leave your bed, do a quiet activity, and return when sleepy.

6. **Serenity Before Sleep**: Create a calming bedtime routine—meditate, read a book, or practice gentle stretches.

7. **Soak Away Stress**: Treat yourself to a warm bath or shower before bedtime to relax.

8. **Tranquil Sanctuary**: Design your sleeping space as a peaceful, tranquil oasis.

9. **Chill Zone**: Keep your sleep space cool for better sleep.

10. **Dim the Lights**: Lower bright light exposure in the evening to signal it's time to wind down.

11. **Tech Timeout**: Power down electronics at least 30 minutes before bed to help your mind unplug.

12. **Nourish Lightly**: If you're hungry before bed, opt for a light, healthy snack.

13. **Energize by Day**: Engage in daytime physical activities to boost energy and improve sleep.

14. **Feast of Balance**: A balanced diet positively impacts sleep quality.

15. **Evening Caffeine Curfew**: Avoid late-day caffeine to ensure it's out of your system by bedtime.

16. **No to Nicotine**: Avoid nicotine before bed for deeper sleep.

17. **Sip Smartly**: Limit alcohol before bed for better rest.

18. **Fluid Moderation**: Reduce fluid intake before sleep to avoid waking up at night.

To effectively implement these sleep hygiene tips, it is advisable to begin by focusing on one or two at first. Gradually, you can incorporate more of them into your routine to ensure a higher quality of sleep. Initially, you might encounter some challenges, such as dealing with uncontrollable noise disruptions. It is a wise approach to brainstorm potential solutions to these issues before initiating your new sleep routine to ensure nothing hinders your restorative rest.

For parents with infants or toddlers, finding a balance can be tricky. First, establishing a sleep routine for the little ones that works for both the children and the parents is crucial. Although achieving a good night's sleep may be challenging, it is vital for parents to prioritize their sleep. Improved sleep not only reduces stress and anxiety levels for parents but also benefits the entire family.

Design Your Room for Better Sleep

The sleep environment you choose plays a crucial role in ensuring a restful night's sleep. Even if you are not consciously aware, a disorganized space can make you feel uncomfortable and impact negatively your sleep quality.

- Declutter: Arrange your sleep space in an organized manner to promote a serene atmosphere.

- Darkness: Minimize light sources in your bedroom to create a dark environment that benefits your circadian rhythm.

- Serenity: Avoid external noise, as it can disrupt your sleep. Avoid having TV noise in the background while you sleep, as it can act as auditory stimulation.

- Comfortable Mattress and Bedding: Invest in a comfortable, well-built mattress to prevent back or neck pain during sleep. Clean, fresh sheets are also crucial for a comfortable sleep experience.

(National Heart Lung and Blood Institute, 2011).

Takeaway

Sleep is a crucial pillar of your overall well-being, with far-reaching effects on various aspects of your lives. The quality of your sleep is closely linked to the timing, duration, and consistency of your sleep routines, as well as your exposure to morning sunlight. Understanding the stages of sleep, such as Non-REM and REM sleep, sheds light on the brain's essential activities during rest. To improve your sleep, implementing sleep hygiene tips can be transformative. Start by focusing on one or two tips and gradually incorporate more into your routine to optimize sleep quality.

Remember to create a tranquil sleep environment and address any challenges that may disrupt your restorative rest. Parents with young children can also find balance by establishing sleep routines that work for both kids and parents. Declutter, embrace darkness, prioritize serenity, and invest in a comfortable mattress and bedding for a truly restful night. By prioritizing quality sleep, we lay a solid foundation for other elements of wellness, such as nutrition, exercise, relaxation, and mental well-being. Improving your sleep can lead to enhanced health, increased energy, and a more positive mood, fostering success in pursuing your life goals.

Chapter 2

Nourishing The Body with Good Nutrition

Chapter Two

Nourishing The Body with Good Nutrition

The second element in this wellness guide is nutrition. The food and drinks you consume each day have a significant impact on your physical health, energy levels, and overall daily performance. According to the U.S. Department of Agriculture, incorporating nutritious ingredients into your diet provides essential vitamins and minerals that support optimal physical activity and brain function. In addition, adopting healthy eating habits can lower the risk of various chronic diseases, such as diabetes and heart disease (Healthy Eating, 2021).

Recent studies also show that a large portion of the population in the United States consumes excessive amounts of sugar and saturated fats. Diets high in these ingredients are associated with weight gain and an increased risk of health complications. Because of this, paying attention to what we eat is not only important for physical health but also for long-term well-being.

Nutrition also plays an important role in mental and emotional health. The brain requires a steady supply of nutrients to function properly. When the body receives balanced nourishment, it can support cognitive functioning, emotional regulation, and stable energy levels throughout the day. On the other hand, poor dietary habits may contribute to fatigue, irritability, and decreased mental performance. For this reason, developing healthy eating habits is an important component of a holistic approach to wellness.

In the realm of nutrition and healthy eating, it is important to pay attention not only to the types of foods you consume but also to the quantity and frequency of your meals. Rather than promoting a specific diet plan, this chapter focuses on the importance of incorporating wholesome ingredients into your daily routine while maintaining moderate and balanced portions. The goal is not perfection, but rather developing sustainable habits that support both physical and mental well-being.

If you are unsure about how healthy your current diet may be, take a moment to reflect on the following questions:

1. Do you drink soda or sugary beverages every day?

2. Do you frequently eat fast food or highly processed meals?

3. Do you often skip fruits and vegetables during the week?

If you answered **"yes"** to any of these questions, this chapter may provide useful guidance for improving your nutrition habits and supporting your overall wellness.

Optimizing Gut Health: Nurturing Your Inner Ecosystem

When discussing factors that contribute to overall well-being, one important element that is often overlooked is gut health. The gastrointestinal tract, commonly referred to as the gut, includes the stomach and intestines, where digestion and nutrient absorption take place. Within this system lives a complex community of microorganisms known as the gut microbiome.

The gut microbiome consists of trillions of bacteria and other microorganisms that play an important role in maintaining the body's balance. These microorganisms help break down food, assist in the absorption of nutrients, and interact with the immune system. In fact, many immune cells communicate with the bacteria in the gut, influencing immune responses and helping the body defend itself against harmful pathogens.

Another important aspect of gut health is the connection between the gut and the brain. Researchers have identified a bidirectional communication system known as the gut–brain axis, which allows the digestive system and the brain to influence one another. The gut microbiota produces neurotransmitters and other bioactive compounds that can affect brain function, mood, and behavior (Järbrink-Sehgal & Andreasson, 2020).

Because of this connection, the condition of the gut can influence aspects of mental health and emotional well-being. Research has shown that the gut microbiome plays a crucial role in overall health and may influence the development of several medical conditions, including celiac disease and type 2 diabetes, among others (Valdes et al., 2018). While many factors contribute to these conditions, maintaining a healthy gut environment is considered an important component of disease prevention and overall wellness.

Supporting gut health involves adopting daily habits that promote balance within the digestive system. Consuming a diet rich in nutritious foods—such as fruits, vegetables, whole grains, and other nutrient-dense ingredients—can help support the growth of beneficial bacteria in the gut. Additionally, lifestyle factors such as managing stress and anxiety can also influence digestive health, since psychological stress can affect gut functioning.

When the gut is functioning properly, it supports digestion, strengthens the immune system, and contributes to improved overall health. Emerging research also suggests that a balanced gut microbiome may play a role in supporting mood regulation and cognitive functioning, highlighting the important relationship between nutrition and mental well-being.

In addition to adopting a nutritious diet, some individuals may consider incorporating probiotics into their routine. Scientific studies indicate that probiotics may offer benefits in managing and preventing certain gastrointestinal disorders (Ritchie & Romanuk, 2012). Probiotics are beneficial live microorganisms, often referred to as "good bacteria"—that can support the balance of the gut microbiome when consumed in adequate amounts.

Probiotics can be found in certain fermented foods, such as yogurt, kefir, sauerkraut, and kimchi. Some people also choose to use probiotic supplements as an additional source. However, because nutritional needs can vary from person to person, it is always advisable to consult with a healthcare professional before starting any new supplement or making significant dietary changes.

Prioritizing gut health can be an important step toward improving both physical and mental wellness. By nourishing the body with balanced nutrition and maintaining healthy lifestyle habits, you can help create an internal environment that supports digestion, immunity, and overall well-being.

Nutrition Basics

To better understand how nutrition supports overall well-being, it is helpful to begin with the basic components of the food we eat. Foods contain a variety of nutrients that the body needs in order to function properly, maintain energy levels, and support both physical and mental health. These nutrients are commonly grouped into two main categories: macronutrients and micronutrients.

According to the U.S. Department of Agriculture, macronutrients are nutrients that the body requires in relatively large amounts. These include carbohydrates, proteins, and fats, which serve as the primary sources of energy for the body and support many essential biological processes. Macronutrients help sustain daily activities, support growth and tissue repair, and allow the body to maintain normal physiological functioning.

Micronutrients, on the other hand, are required in smaller quantities but are equally important for maintaining health. These nutrients include vitamins and minerals that assist in a wide range of bodily functions, such as immune defense, cellular repair, nerve communication, and metabolic regulation.

Achieving a balanced intake of both macronutrients and micronutrients is essential for maintaining optimal health and supporting overall wellness. When the body receives a consistent supply of these nutrients through a varied and balanced diet, it is better equipped to perform its daily functions, maintain stable energy levels, and support long-term health.

Understanding the role that nutrients play in the body can help individuals make more informed choices about the foods they consume. Rather than focusing on restrictive diets or short-term trends, it can be more helpful to think about nutrition as a way of nourishing the body and supporting its natural functions. Over time, developing awareness of these basic nutritional components can help guide healthier food choices and promote a more balanced approach to eating.

Macronutrients

To promote both longevity and overall well-being, it is important to include a balanced combination of macronutrients in the daily diet (Venn, 2020). Each macronutrient plays a unique role in supporting the body's structure, energy needs, and internal processes. When consumed in appropriate amounts, these nutrients work together to support physical health, mental performance, and overall vitality.

Carbohydrates

Carbohydrates are one of the body's primary sources of energy. During digestion, carbohydrates are broken down into glucose, which the body uses as fuel for many biological processes. Glucose is especially important for the brain, which relies on a steady supply of energy in order to support concentration, memory, and cognitive functioning.

Foods that contain carbohydrates include whole grains, bread, fruits, vegetables, beans, and dairy products. Many of these foods also provide important nutrients such as fiber, vitamins, and minerals that support digestive health and overall well-being. Consuming carbohydrate-rich foods that are minimally processed can help promote stable energy levels throughout the day and contribute to a feeling of satiety after meals.

Proteins

Proteins play a critical role in the growth, repair, and maintenance of body tissues. They are composed of amino acids, which serve as building blocks for muscles, organs, enzymes, and hormones. Protein also contributes to immune system function and helps the body recover from physical activity or injury.

Common sources of protein include meat, poultry, seafood, eggs, dairy products, soy products, beans, legumes, nuts, and seeds. Including adequate amounts of protein in daily meals can help support muscle health, maintain energy levels, and promote a feeling of fullness that may assist in balanced eating habits.

Fats

Dietary fats are another essential macronutrient that supports many important functions in the body. When consumed, fats are broken down into fatty acids and glycerol, which the body can use for energy storage and cellular functions. Fats also help transport and absorb fat-soluble vitamins such as vitamins A, D, E, and K.

Foods that contain healthy fats include avocados, nuts, seeds, olive oil, and certain dairy products. Including moderate amounts of healthy fats in the diet can support heart health, brain function, and overall nutritional balance.

When striving to eat in a healthier way, it can be helpful to focus on foods that are closer to their natural state. Whole foods that are minimally processed often provide a more balanced combination of macronutrients and micronutrients. Fruits, vegetables, whole grains, lean proteins, and healthy fats all contribute valuable nutrients that support the body's daily functioning.

A balanced intake of macronutrients also supports digestive health. The nutrients found in these foods help maintain the body's internal systems, including the digestive tract and the microorganisms that live within it. As discussed earlier in the chapter, supporting digestive health can contribute to better nutrient absorption, a stronger immune system, and improved overall well-being, including aspects related to mental health.

Micronutrients

Micronutrients refer to the vitamins and minerals found in the foods we eat and, in some cases, in dietary supplements. Although the body requires these nutrients in smaller amounts than macronutrients, they are essential for maintaining proper physiological functioning. Unlike some other substances produced naturally in the body, many micronutrients must be obtained through food sources. For this reason, they are often referred to as essential nutrients.

Vitamins and minerals play an important role in supporting many biological processes. They contribute to immune function, help regulate metabolism, assist with cellular repair, and support the proper functioning of the nervous system. Because of their involvement in so many bodily systems, an adequate intake of micronutrients is necessary for maintaining both physical and mental well-being.

Micronutrients also play a significant role in the body's immune response. Vitamins and minerals help regulate the activity of immune cells and assist the body in defending itself against infections and other health threats. Research has shown that individuals across different age groups may experience deficiencies in certain micronutrients. When these deficiencies occur, the body's ability to maintain optimal immune function may be affected. In some cases, appropriate supplementation may help support immune responses and overall health (Pecora, Persico, Argentiero, Neglia, & Esposito, 2020).

According to the National Institutes of Health (NIH), a variety of vitamins and minerals are considered essential for maintaining good health (National Institutes of Health Office of Dietary Supplements, n.d.). These nutrients support a wide range of biological functions that allow the body to grow, repair itself, and maintain internal balance.

Examples of Vitamins and Their Functions

Below are examples of several important vitamins and some of the foods in which they can be found.

Vitamin A supports immune function and helps maintain proper vision. It can be found in foods such as beef liver, fish, eggs, and dairy products.

Vitamin C plays an important role in the formation of collagen and the production of certain neurotransmitters. It is commonly found in citrus fruits, red and green peppers, tomatoes, and broccoli.

Vitamin D helps the body absorb calcium and supports bone growth and bone health. Sources include fatty fish, eggs, and certain types of mushrooms.

Vitamin E acts as an antioxidant that helps protect cells from damage caused by oxidative stress. It also supports immune system functioning. Foods rich in vitamin E include nuts and seeds.

Vitamin K is necessary for the production of proteins involved in blood clotting and bone health. It can be found in green leafy vegetables and certain fruits such as blueberries and grapes.

B Vitamins (B1, B2, B3, B5, B6, B7, B9, and B12) The B vitamins function as a group of nutrients that support several essential processes in the body. They contribute to energy metabolism, support the health of blood and nerve cells, assist in cell growth and development, and play an important role in the production of DNA and other genetic material. Foods that contain B vitamins include leafy green vegetables, dairy products, animal proteins, and beans.

In addition to vitamins, minerals are another essential group of micronutrients. Minerals help regulate important bodily processes, including nerve transmission, muscle contraction, fluid balance, and immune system function.

According to the NIH, essential minerals include calcium, phosphorus, magnesium, sodium, chloride, potassium, sulfur, iron, manganese, copper, zinc, iodine, fluoride, and selenium (National Institutes of Health Office of Dietary Supplements, n.d.). These minerals support a variety of physiological processes that allow the body to maintain balance and function efficiently.

Because micronutrients are found in many different foods, consuming a varied and balanced diet is one of the most effective ways to ensure the body receives the nutrients it needs. Fruits, vegetables, whole grains, legumes, dairy products, and protein sources all contribute important vitamins and minerals that support overall health.

Maintaining adequate levels of micronutrients helps support immune function, protect cells from damage, and promote proper functioning of the body's organs and systems. When the body receives sufficient vitamins and minerals through nutrition, it is better able to maintain balance and support both physical and mental well-being.

Nutritionally Poor Food Choices

The body and mind respond to the types of foods that are consumed on a regular basis. Choosing foods that are rich in nutrients can support energy levels, strengthen the immune system, and contribute to an overall sense of well-being. In contrast, diets that are consistently low in essential nutrients may gradually affect physical health and increase the risk of long-term health complications.

Foods that are highly processed often contain large amounts of added sugars, unhealthy fats, sodium, and artificial ingredients while providing relatively few essential nutrients. When these foods are consumed frequently, they may contribute to weight gain, inflammation, and other health concerns that can negatively affect the body over time.

Research suggests that reducing the consumption of certain types of foods may help lower the risk of developing various chronic diseases. These foods include processed meats, trans fats, excessive saturated fats, sugary beverages, refined grains, and foods that contain high levels of added sugars (Cena & Calder, 2020). Diets that rely heavily on these types of foods have been associated with an increased risk of cardiovascular disease, metabolic disorders, and other health conditions.

In addition to physical health effects, dietary patterns may also influence how people feel on a daily basis. Diets that are high in added sugars and heavily processed ingredients may contribute to fluctuations in energy levels and may affect concentration and mood. On the other hand, diets that emphasize whole foods and balanced nutrition tend to support more stable energy levels and better overall functioning.

This does not mean that every food choice must be perfect or that occasional indulgences should be avoided entirely. A balanced approach to nutrition allows room for flexibility while still prioritizing foods that provide essential nutrients. The goal is to develop habits that emphasize nourishing the body most of the time, rather than striving for strict or unrealistic dietary rules.

By becoming more aware of the nutritional quality of foods and making gradual improvements in dietary habits, individuals can support both their physical health and their overall well-being. Choosing foods that are closer to their natural state, such as fruits, vegetables, whole grains, and lean protein sources, can help provide the body with the nutrients it needs to function effectively.

The Importance of Hydration

Proper hydration is an essential aspect of overall nutrition and plays an important role in maintaining the body's normal functioning. Staying adequately hydrated means consuming enough fluids throughout the day, particularly water, to support the body's many physiological processes. Water is involved in several critical functions, including regulating body temperature, transporting nutrients, supporting digestion, and helping remove waste products from the body.

Research suggests that maintaining adequate hydration can contribute to several health benefits. These include supporting healthy blood pressure levels, regulating body temperature, assisting in the removal of waste materials, and helping protect kidney function over time (Nakamura et al., 2020). Because water supports so many biological processes, maintaining proper hydration can also contribute to better physical performance and improved cognitive functioning.

While water is the most common and effective way to stay hydrated, fluids can also come from other beverages and certain foods that contain a high-water content. Fruits, vegetables, soups, and broths can all contribute to daily hydration and support the body's fluid balance.

Although most people understand the importance of drinking water, many individuals still struggle to consume enough fluids throughout the day. Busy schedules, forgetfulness, or a dislike of plain water can make it difficult to maintain consistent hydration habits. Fortunately, there are several simple strategies that can help make drinking water easier and more enjoyable.

Ideas to Help You Drink More Water

• Add slices of fruit, such as lemon, lime, or berries, to your water to create a refreshing flavor.
• Set reminders on your phone or create small routines throughout the day to encourage regular water intake.
• Carry a reusable water bottle with you when leaving the house so that water is readily available.
• Drink water during meals instead of sugary beverages whenever possible.

Overcoming Common Barriers to Hydration

Busy schedule:

Daily responsibilities can make it easy to forget to drink water. Setting reminders on a phone or placing a water bottle nearby during work or daily activities can serve as helpful cues to drink fluids regularly throughout the day.

Dislike of plain water:

Some individuals find plain water unappealing. In these cases, adding natural flavors such as fresh fruit, cucumber, or herbs can make water more enjoyable. Herbal teas can also be a hydrating alternative, as they typically do not contain caffeine and contribute to daily fluid intake.

Alternative hydrating beverages:

Other beverages, such as coconut water or electrolyte drinks that do not contain artificial coloring or excessive sugar, may also help support hydration in certain situations. However, water should remain the primary source of daily fluid intake for most individuals.

In addition to beverages, incorporating water-rich foods into meals can also support hydration. Fruits such as watermelon, strawberries, and pineapple, as well as vegetables like cucumber, naturally contain high amounts of water. Soups and broths are additional options that can help increase fluid intake throughout the day.

Maintaining adequate hydration is a simple but powerful way to support overall health. When the body receives enough fluids, it is better able to regulate temperature, support brain function, assist digestion, and maintain healthy circulation. By becoming mindful of daily fluid intake and adopting small habits that encourage hydration, individuals can support both their physical health and their overall well-being.

Practical Tips for Healthy Nutrition Habits

Understanding Nutrition Facts Labels

Nutrition facts labels can be a valuable tool for individuals who want to make more informed food choices. These labels provide information about the nutritional content of packaged foods and help consumers better understand what they are putting into their bodies. Learning how to read and interpret these labels can empower individuals to select foods that better support their health and overall well-being.

Although nutrition labels may appear complicated at first, they are designed to present information in a standardized format that allows consumers to easily compare products. By becoming familiar with a few key components of the label, individuals can begin to make more thoughtful decisions about the foods they purchase and consume.

Serving Size

One of the first things to examine on a nutrition label is the **serving size**. The serving size indicates the amount of food that the nutritional information is based on. Many packaged foods contain more than one serving per container, which means the nutritional values listed on the label apply only to the specified portion.

For example, a package of snacks might appear to be a single serving but actually contain two or three servings. If a person consumes the entire package, they may be consuming two or three times the calories, sugar, sodium, or fat listed on the label. Paying attention to serving size can help individuals better understand how much they are actually eating.

Calories

Calories represent the amount of energy a food provides to the body. The calorie information listed on a nutrition label indicates how much energy is contained in a single serving of that product.

While calories are an important consideration, they should not be the only factor used when evaluating a food. Foods that are high in nutrients, such as fruits, vegetables, whole grains, and lean proteins, may contain calories but also provide vitamins, minerals, and other nutrients that support health. Focusing only on calories can sometimes lead individuals to overlook the overall nutritional quality of a food.

Nutrients to Monitor

Nutrition labels also list several nutrients that individuals may want to monitor or limit as part of a balanced diet. These typically include saturated fat, sodium, and added sugars. Consuming these nutrients in excessive amounts over time has been associated with increased health risks, including cardiovascular disease and other chronic conditions.

By reviewing these values on food labels, individuals can become more aware of how much of these nutrients they are consuming and make adjustments when necessary.

Nutrients to Prioritize

In addition to identifying nutrients that should be limited, nutrition labels can also highlight nutrients that support overall health. These often include dietary fiber, vitamins, and minerals such as calcium, iron, and potassium.

Choosing foods that provide beneficial nutrients can help support many bodily functions, including digestion, bone health, and immune functioning. Over time, prioritizing foods that contain these nutrients can contribute to a more balanced and nourishing diet.

Percent Daily Value

Another helpful feature of nutrition labels is the Percent Daily Value (%DV). This percentage indicates how much a particular nutrient in one serving contributes to the recommended daily intake based on a standard 2,000-calorie diet.

As a general guideline, a 5% Daily Value or less is considered low for a nutrient, while 20% Daily Value or more is considered high. This information can help individuals quickly determine whether a food contains a small or large amount of a particular nutrient.

For example, a food that provides 20% of the Daily Value for fiber may be a good source of fiber, while a food that provides 20% of the Daily Value for sodium may contain a relatively high amount of sodium.

Using Labels to Support Healthier Choices

Learning how to read nutrition labels does not mean that individuals must analyze every food item they encounter. Instead, the goal is to develop a general awareness of the nutritional content of foods and to use that knowledge when making everyday choices.

Over time, this awareness can help individuals select foods that better align with their health goals. By paying attention to serving sizes, calories, and key nutrients, consumers can develop a clearer understanding of what they are eating and how those foods may support their overall well-being.

Grocery Shopping

Grocery shopping plays an important role in maintaining healthy eating habits. The foods that individuals bring into their homes often influence the choices they make throughout the week. By approaching grocery shopping with intention and planning, people can create an environment that supports healthier eating patterns.

One helpful strategy is to plan meals ahead of time before going to the store. Taking a few minutes to think about meals for the upcoming days can make shopping more focused and efficient. Creating a shopping list based on those planned meals helps reduce impulse purchases and ensures that the necessary ingredients are available at home.

Another useful approach is to focus on whole and minimally processed foods whenever possible. Fresh fruits, vegetables, whole grains, lean proteins, nuts, and legumes provide many of the nutrients the body needs to function well. Including a variety of these foods in the grocery cart can help support balanced meals throughout the week.

Many grocery stores are designed so that perishable foods such as produce, dairy, and meats are located around the perimeter of the store, while more heavily processed foods are often found in the center aisles. While there are healthy options in every part of the store, spending more time selecting foods from the outer sections can help increase the likelihood of purchasing fresh and nutrient-dense items.

Reading nutrition facts labels and ingredient lists can also be helpful when comparing packaged foods. Becoming familiar with serving sizes, added sugars, sodium content, and other nutrients can support more informed decisions when selecting products.

Finally, it can be helpful to avoid grocery shopping when extremely hungry. Hunger can make highly processed or convenience foods more tempting and may lead to purchasing items that were not originally planned. Eating a small meal or snack before shopping can help individuals stay focused on their list and make more intentional choices.

Grocery shopping does not have to be complicated or restrictive. Instead, it can be viewed as an opportunity to choose foods that support health and well-being. Over time, small and consistent decisions at the grocery store can make it easier to maintain balanced eating habits at home.

Meal Planning

Meal planning is another practical strategy that can support healthier eating habits. By taking some time to plan meals in advance, individuals can reduce the stress that often comes with deciding what to eat at the last minute. Planning ahead can also make it easier to include a variety of nutritious foods throughout the week.

One of the benefits of meal planning is that it encourages individuals to think about balance when preparing meals. A balanced meal often includes a combination of lean protein, whole grains or other complex carbohydrates, healthy fats, and fruits or vegetables. When meals contain a mix of these components, they are more likely to provide sustained energy and a range of nutrients that support the body's needs.

Meal planning can also help people save time and reduce food waste. Preparing a weekly plan allows individuals to purchase only the ingredients they need, which can prevent unused foods from spoiling. Some people also find it helpful to prepare certain ingredients in advance, such as chopping vegetables, cooking grains, or preparing protein sources that can be used in multiple meals throughout the week.

It is important to remember that meal planning does not require rigid rules or perfectly structured meals. Flexibility is key. Unexpected schedule changes or shifting preferences may require adjustments, and that is completely normal. The goal of meal planning is simply to create a helpful structure that makes nourishing choices easier.

For individuals who are new to meal planning, starting small can be helpful. Planning just a few meals for the week or preparing ingredients for two or three days at a time can make the process feel more manageable. As people become more comfortable with the practice, they may gradually expand their planning to cover additional meals.

Ultimately, meal planning is not about perfection. Rather, it is about creating supportive routines that make healthy eating more accessible in everyday life. With time and practice, this simple habit can help individuals feel more organized, reduce daily decision-making around food, and support overall well-being.

Building a Balanced Diet: Nutritious and Delicious Recipes

Based on the food groups and healthy ingredients discussed throughout this chapter, individuals can explore a wide variety of meal options that support both physical and mental well-being. Building a balanced diet does not require complicated recipes or strict rules. Instead, it involves combining nutritious ingredients in ways that are both satisfying and enjoyable.

Meals that include a balance of whole grains, lean proteins, healthy fats, and fruits or vegetables can help provide the body with sustained energy and a wide range of essential nutrients. These foods support many important bodily functions, including digestion, immune health, and brain function.

The following sample menu offers simple meal ideas that incorporate many of the ingredients discussed earlier in the chapter. These suggestions are meant to serve as examples rather than rigid guidelines. Individuals are encouraged to adjust ingredients, substitute foods, or modify recipes according to their preferences, cultural traditions, and dietary needs.

It is important to be mindful of food allergies or medical conditions that may affect dietary choices. If you have a food allergy or specific nutritional concerns, avoid ingredients that may trigger a reaction and consult a healthcare professional for personalized guidance.

Adapting Healthy Eating to Your Culture and Traditions

Healthy eating does not require abandoning the foods that are part of your culture or family traditions. In many cases, traditional cuisines around the world already include many nutritious ingredients such as vegetables, legumes, whole grains, herbs, and natural sources of protein.

Rather than following a specific meal plan, individuals can focus on incorporating the principles discussed throughout this chapter into the foods they already enjoy. For example, meals can include a balance of protein, whole grains or other complex carbohydrates, healthy fats, and fruits or vegetables. Many traditional dishes already contain these components when prepared with whole ingredients.

For individuals from different cultural backgrounds, healthy eating may look different depending on the foods commonly prepared in their homes and communities. A person from the Caribbean, Latin America, Asia, Africa, or Europe may prepare meals using different ingredients, spices, and cooking methods. These differences are part of the richness of cultural food traditions and can still support good nutrition.

In many cases, traditional home-cooked meals prepared with minimally processed ingredients may offer nutritional benefits compared to highly processed convenience foods. By focusing on whole ingredients, balanced portions, and mindful preparation, individuals can maintain their cultural food traditions while still supporting their health and well-being.

Ultimately, healthy eating is not about following a single universal menu. Instead, it is about understanding the principles of balanced nutrition and applying them in ways that align with one's culture, preferences, and lifestyle.

Takeaway

Nutrition plays a meaningful role in supporting both physical and mental well-being. The foods we consume provide the body with the nutrients needed to sustain energy, support brain function, and maintain overall health. Research has shown that diets high in excessive added sugars and saturated fats may contribute to weight gain and increase the risk of various chronic health conditions. For this reason, prioritizing nutrient-dense foods can be an important step toward improving long-term health.

One important aspect of nutrition involves supporting the health of the gut microbiome, the complex community of microorganisms that live in the digestive system. The gut microbiome plays a role in digestion, metabolism, immune functioning, and even aspects of mental health. When the balance of this system is disrupted, it may contribute to gastrointestinal discomfort and other health concerns. Consuming a variety of whole foods, including fruits, vegetables, whole grains, and sources of fiber, can help support a healthy gut environment.

Adequate hydration is another important component of overall wellness. Drinking enough fluids throughout the day helps regulate body temperature, support cognitive performance, and assist the body in maintaining normal physiological processes. Simple habits such as keeping water nearby and incorporating water-rich foods into meals can help individuals stay properly hydrated.

In addition to what we eat, how we approach food also matters. Practicing mindful eating can encourage individuals to become more aware of their food choices, hunger cues, and eating patterns. This awareness can help people develop a healthier relationship with food while making choices that align with their well-being.

Healthy eating does not have to be restrictive or repetitive. There are countless ways to prepare nourishing meals using a variety of ingredients and flavors. Exploring new recipes, planning meals, and preparing food at home can become enjoyable activities that support both health and creativity. For some individuals, cooking can even serve as a relaxing and rewarding way to step away from daily stress.

By incorporating balanced meals, staying hydrated, planning ahead, and approaching food with greater awareness, individuals can create sustainable habits that support both their physical health and their mental well-being.

Chapter 3
The Power of Exercise

72

Chapter Three

The Power of Exercise

The third element in *The Wellness Guide* is exercise, which simply means staying physically active. Sometimes exercise is seen as a luxury—something people do only if they have extra time—rather than a vital priority. However, regular movement does much more than change how your body looks. It supports your physical health and can also have a powerful effect on your mental well-being. In this way, exercise works together with the other elements presented in this book, strengthening your overall wellness.

Physical activity has always been a natural part of human life. In the past, early humans moved far more than we typically do today because their daily survival depended on it. Walking long distances, gathering food, building shelter, and hunting required constant physical effort. Movement was not considered "exercise"; it was simply part of living.

In contrast, modern life often prioritizes convenience. Technology, transportation, and sedentary work have greatly reduced the amount of movement built into our daily routines. Many people can go through an entire day with very little physical activity. Although our lifestyles have changed, our bodies have not. The human body is designed to move, and when movement becomes limited, both physical and mental well-being can be affected.

Exercise, therefore, is not simply an optional activity for improving appearance. It is an essential component of maintaining health and supporting a balanced sense of well-being. Engaging in regular physical activity can strengthen the body, support brain function, and contribute to a greater sense of vitality in daily life.

If you are unsure about your current level of physical activity, consider reflecting on the following questions:

1. Do you regularly engage in physical activities such as exercise, sports, or outdoor movement?

2. Do you generally feel physically capable of completing your daily tasks without excessive fatigue?

3. Do you spend at least 30 minutes most days of the week engaging in some form of physical activity?

If you answered "no" to one or more of these questions, the information in this chapter may help you explore ways to incorporate more movement into your routine.

Note: Before beginning any new exercise program, it is advisable to consult with a healthcare professional, particularly if you have underlying health conditions or concerns. A qualified physical trainer can also help tailor an exercise plan that fits your individual needs and abilities.

Sedentary Lifestyle

In today's technology-driven world, many people find themselves living increasingly sedentary lives. Modern conveniences have made everyday tasks easier than ever before, but they have also quietly reduced the amount of movement in our daily routines. Groceries can be delivered to our door, entertainment can be streamed for hours, and conversations with friends often take place through screens rather than face-to-face interactions. While these innovations offer undeniable benefits, they can also encourage long periods of sitting and inactivity.

As a result, many individuals move far less than previous generations did. Work, transportation, and leisure activities often revolve around sitting, at desks, in cars, or on couches. What once required movement and physical effort can now be done with the tap of a screen. Although these changes may seem harmless in the moment, over time they can lead to a significant decline in daily physical activity.

The effects of this shift toward sedentary living are becoming increasingly clear. Research suggests that prolonged inactivity can affect both physical and mental health. In fact, a review of 12 prospective studies found a significant association between sedentary behaviors, particularly mentally passive activities, and an increased risk of depression. For example, spending extended periods on a computer or engaging in passive screen time may reduce opportunities for social interaction and physical movement, which can contribute to depressive symptoms over time (Huang et al., 2020). These findings highlight the importance of becoming more aware of how sedentary habits may influence overall well-being.

To better understand how a sedentary lifestyle can develop, consider a common scenario experienced by many adults today. A typical workday may involve sitting at a computer for eight or more hours, often with few breaks for movement. Lunch might be eaten quickly at the desk while continuing to work, and by the end of the day, fatigue makes it tempting to relax on the couch rather than engage in physical activity. Over time, this routine can become the norm.

When daily movement becomes limited, several aspects of well-being may begin to change. Energy levels may decline, sleep may feel less restorative, and stress can accumulate more easily. Without regular opportunities for the body to move and release tension, both physical and emotional strain may gradually build.

The encouraging news is that meaningful change does not always require dramatic lifestyle shifts. Even small adjustments can begin to reverse sedentary patterns. Some people start by taking short walks during the day, stretching between tasks, or dedicating a brief period of time to movement after work. Others choose to involve family members by going on evening walks, playing outside with their children, or exploring outdoor activities together.

These small moments of movement can gradually lead to noticeable improvements. Many people report feeling more energized, experiencing better sleep, and finding it easier to manage daily stress when regular physical activity becomes part of their routine. The goal is not perfection or intense training, but simply reconnecting with the natural movement that the body was designed for.

What Happens When you Exercise: Physiology and Benefits

When you begin to move your body, a series of coordinated processes immediately take place. As you breathe in, oxygen enters your lungs and travels through your bloodstream to your muscles. This oxygen helps your muscles produce the energy they need to keep moving. At the same time, your heart begins to beat faster, pumping oxygen-rich blood throughout your body so your muscles can continue working efficiently (Muise, Gordon, & Ericson Woods, 2021).

As your level of activity increases, your body adjusts to meet the growing demand for energy. Your breathing becomes deeper and more frequent, allowing more oxygen to enter your bloodstream. Your heart rate rises to circulate that oxygen more quickly, while your body works to remove waste products such as carbon dioxide that are produced during physical activity

(Muise, Gordon, & Ericson Woods, 2021). You may notice sensations such as warmth, sweating, or mild muscle fatigue. These responses are natural signs that your body is actively working to support movement.

With consistent physical activity, the body gradually becomes more efficient at performing these processes. Over time, the heart and lungs grow stronger, allowing them to deliver oxygen more effectively. Muscles also adapt, becoming better at using energy and sustaining activity for longer periods of time.

This ability to adapt is one of the remarkable features of the human body. Each time you engage in physical activity, you are gently training your body to function more efficiently. Gradually, activities that once felt tiring may begin to feel easier, allowing you to move through your day with greater strength, stamina, and energy.

Brain and Exercise

Research suggests that regular physical activity can play an important role in supporting brain health and slowing aspects of brain aging. Exercise has been associated with improvements in cognitive functions such as memory, attention, and mental flexibility. Although scientists have long observed these benefits, the biological mechanisms behind them are still being explored.

Recent research examining the effects of exercise on brain cells has provided helpful insights. In studies conducted with mice, researchers found that physical activity influenced several types of aging brain cells, making their characteristics more similar to those found in younger brains. Exercise was also associated with a reduction in certain immune cells that tend to accumulate in the aging brain. These changes suggest that regular movement may support healthier brain function at a cellular level and help maintain cognitive abilities as we age (Chauquet et al., 2024).

While more research continues to explore these mechanisms, the findings reinforce an important idea: staying physically active can be a meaningful way to support long-term brain health.

Mental Benefits of Exercise

Regular physical activity is associated with several benefits for mental well-being, including:

- Reduced stress and anxiety

- Improved mood
- Better cognitive functioning and memory
- Increased self-confidence and self-esteem

Researchers have also begun examining how exercise interacts with other lifestyle factors that influence mental health. A recent study explored the relationship between physical activity, diet, and lifestyle habits in managing anxiety among college students. The study surveyed 498 students from three universities in Fujian, China, to better understand how these factors worked together to influence anxiety levels (Sun, Zhu, & Bao, 2024).

The findings showed that regular physical activity was associated with lower levels of anxiety. However, the benefits were even greater when exercise was combined with other healthy lifestyle habits and balanced nutrition. The researchers found that lifestyle and dietary habits accounted for 24.9% of the anxiety-reducing effects of exercise, while the combination of these factors contributed an additional 13.27%. In total, exercise and related lifestyle factors accounted for 36.93% of the reduction in anxiety symptoms observed among the students (Sun, Zhu, & Bao, 2024).

These findings highlight an important point. Exercise does not occur in isolation. Its benefits often become stronger when it is part of a broader pattern of healthy living that includes good nutrition, adequate sleep, and supportive daily habits.

When thinking about your own routine, it may be helpful to view exercise as one part of a larger wellness system. Physical movement, balanced nutrition, and healthy lifestyle choices can work together to support both physical and mental well-being.

Increasing physical activity has also been associated with a lower prevalence of certain mental health conditions, particularly anxiety and depression. Individuals experiencing mental health challenges sometimes face disparities in physical health, partly due to lower levels of physical activity and other lifestyle factors. Research suggests that incorporating regular movement into daily routines can help support improvements in overall well-being and may contribute to reductions in some mental health symptoms (Schuch & Vancampfort, 2021).

Additional research with university students provides further support for this connection. In an online study involving male and female students with no history of psychiatric disorders, those who reported engaging in regular physical activity also reported lower levels of depression, anxiety, and stress. They also described a higher quality of life in areas such as physical health, general well-being, and social relationships (Herbert, Meixner, Wiebking, & Gilg, 2020). These findings suggest a meaningful relationship between regular movement and improved overall well-being, even among individuals who spend significant portions of their day sitting.

One reason exercise may support brain function relates to a remarkable feature of the human brain known as **neuroplasticity**, the brain's ability to adapt and change over time. Neuroplasticity allows neurons to modify their connections in response to experiences and environmental stimuli. Researchers have also discovered that the adult brain can generate new neurons, a process known as neurogenesis.

Physical activity appears to support these processes. Studies suggest that exercise may stimulate the release of certain substances produced by muscles during movement that influence brain signaling pathways. These signals can help strengthen connections between neurons and support functions such as memory, learning, and attention (Di Liegro et al., 2019).

Take a moment to reflect on your own experience with physical activity. Think about the last time you went for a walk, exercised, or engaged in a form of movement you enjoy. During that time, your body and brain were working together in ways you may not have noticed. As your muscles moved, your brain was also responding by activating chemical signals that help support concentration, learning, and mental clarity.

You might consider reflecting on the following questions:

1. After engaging in physical activity, do you notice changes in your ability to concentrate or think clearly?

2. When you feel mentally fatigued or unfocused, could a short period of movement help refresh your attention?

Even small moments of activity, such as a brief walk or light exercise, may help support the brain's ability to adapt and function effectively.

Physical exercise can also influence how individuals view themselves and interact with others. Engaging in regular physical activity may contribute to improvements in self-esteem by helping people feel more confident in their physical abilities and by providing a sense of progress and accomplishment.

Research suggests that these changes in self-perception can also influence social and emotional functioning. Individuals who participate in regular exercise often report greater social adaptability and confidence when interacting with others. Physical activity may also support social-emotional skills by helping individuals manage their emotions and respond more effectively to social situations.

As emotional regulation and self-confidence improve, individuals may feel more comfortable navigating relationships and adapting to new environments. These changes can contribute to stronger social connections and a greater sense of resilience in everyday life. Research findings suggest that encouraging regular physical activity may support not only physical health but also emotional well-being and social functioning (Liu, Feng, Tong, & Guo, 2023).

Physical Benefits of Exercise

Regular physical activity provides a wide range of physical health benefits, including:

- Improved sleep

- Increased energy
- Better cardiovascular health
- Support for healthy weight management
- Increased strength and endurance
- Reduced risk of chronic diseases

One area where exercise appears to have a particularly meaningful impact is sleep. Exercise is often recommended as a supportive strategy for improving sleep quality. In one research study, 80 sedentary adults with chronic primary insomnia, between the ages of 35 and 56, were randomly assigned to either a supervised aerobic exercise group or a control group (Abd El-Kader & Al-Jiffri, 2020).

Researchers evaluated sleep quality using polysomnographic recordings, a method that measures various physiological signals in the brain and body during sleep. Psychological well-being and immune system markers were also assessed using tools such as the Beck Depression Inventory, the Profile of Mood States, the Rosenberg Self-Esteem Scale, and blood tests (Abd El-Kader & Al-Jiffri, 2020). These measurements were taken before the intervention and again after six months.

The results showed that participants who engaged in regular aerobic exercise experienced noticeable improvements in several aspects of sleep. They slept longer, fell asleep more quickly, and reported better overall sleep quality compared with their baseline results. In addition, participants in the exercise group showed reductions in depressive symptoms and mood disturbances, along with increases in self-esteem and improvements in certain immune system markers (Abd El-Kader & Al-Jiffri, 2020).

Exercise does not always require long or demanding workouts to produce meaningful benefits. Another study found that incorporating just three minutes of intense exercise within a 30-minute training session could significantly improve both muscle health and cardiovascular function (Gillen et al., 2014). This finding suggests that even relatively short periods of physical activity can support overall health.

For individuals who feel intimidated by the idea of exercising for long periods, this can be encouraging. Exercise does not have to begin with an hour-long routine. Starting with 30 minutes of movement and gradually increasing activity over time can be a practical and sustainable way to build healthier habits.

Conquering Obstacles to Exercise

When people decide to become more physically active, they often encounter obstacles that make it difficult to maintain consistency. Good intentions alone do not always translate into lasting habits. Many individuals begin with motivation and clear goals, yet everyday challenges can interfere with their ability to follow through.

In my work as a therapist, I often encourage clients to incorporate regular physical activity as part of a healthy lifestyle, both during and after therapy. While many express a genuine desire to become more active, they frequently encounter practical barriers that make it difficult to maintain their intentions. Common challenges include finding time, managing physical discomfort, or struggling with low energy after long days. These experiences are very common and do not mean a person lacks motivation or discipline.

Recognizing these challenges can be an important first step. Below are several common obstacles people face when trying to exercise regularly, along with practical ways to address them.

Lack of Time

One of the most frequently reported barriers to exercise is a perceived lack of time. Work responsibilities, family obligations, and daily tasks can make it feel difficult to fit physical activity into an already busy schedule.

One helpful approach is to intentionally schedule exercise as part of your daily routine. Physical activity does not always need to occur in long sessions. Shorter periods of movement throughout the day, such as brief walks or short exercise routines, can still provide meaningful benefits and may feel more manageable.

Physical Discomfort

Some individuals experience muscle soreness or physical discomfort when they begin exercising, particularly if they have been inactive for a long period of time. This can make the initial stages of developing an exercise routine feel discouraging.

Starting gradually and paying attention to your body's signals can help prevent excessive strain. Low-impact activities, such as walking, stretching, swimming, or gentle cycling, can be good starting points. If discomfort persists or if there are existing health concerns, consulting a healthcare professional can help ensure that the chosen activities are appropriate and safe.

Unrealistic Expectations

Setting overly ambitious goals can sometimes lead to frustration and discouragement. When progress does not happen as quickly as expected, it may be tempting to give up altogether.

Instead, consider starting with small and achievable goals. Gradually increasing the duration or intensity of exercise can help build confidence and make progress feel more attainable. Writing down these goals and tracking small improvements over time can serve as a helpful reminder of the progress being made.

Monotony and Boredom

Repeating the same type of exercise every day can eventually feel monotonous, which may reduce motivation over time. When physical activity becomes predictable or uninteresting, it can be harder to maintain consistency.

Adding variety to your routine can help keep exercise enjoyable. Trying different activities, exploring new workout formats, or participating in group classes can bring a sense of novelty and engagement. Some people also find it helpful to listen to music, podcasts, or audiobooks while exercising to make the experience more enjoyable.

Lack of Sleep

Sleep quality can strongly influence a person's ability to stay physically active. Individuals who experience poor sleep or insomnia often feel fatigued during the day, which can make exercise feel more difficult.

As discussed in the previous chapter on sleep, maintaining good sleep hygiene can help improve energy levels and overall well-being. Aim for at least seven hours of uninterrupted sleep whenever possible. When the body receives adequate rest, it is easier to wake up feeling refreshed and ready to engage in physical activity during the day.

Consistency Over Perfection

Like many habits, exercise often comes with the misconception that every workout must be done perfectly. Some people believe that missing a day or falling short of a specific goal means they have failed. In reality, meaningful progress rarely comes from perfection. It comes from consistency.

Life does not always allow for ideal conditions. Busy schedules, low energy, unexpected responsibilities, or demanding days can interfere with even the best intentions. What truly matters is continuing to engage with physical activity whenever possible, even if the effort is smaller than originally planned. A short walk, a brief stretch, or a few minutes of movement can still contribute to maintaining the habit.

Over time, consistent effort helps build strength, endurance, and resilience. In contrast, striving for perfection can sometimes lead to frustration or burnout when expectations are not met. Consistency and discipline gradually strengthen not only the body but also a person's sense of self-trust. Each time you follow through on a commitment to move your body, you reinforce your confidence in your ability to stay dedicated to your goals.

Consider how people learn new skills. When someone begins learning to play the piano, they do not expect to master the instrument in a single day. Progress happens through regular practice, even when the sessions are short or imperfect. Each repetition builds familiarity and skill over time. Exercise works in a similar way. Small, consistent actions gradually create lasting change.

Even on days when motivation is low, choosing to move in some way can help maintain momentum. A shorter workout or a simple stretch can still support your long-term goals. What matters most is continuing the practice of showing up for yourself.

Tips for Staying Consistent:

1. Find a workout partner: Exercising with someone else can increase accountability and make the experience more enjoyable.

2. Allow room for missed days: If you miss a workout, try not to view it as failure. Simply return to your routine the next day.

3. Track your progress: Keeping a simple record of your activity, even brief sessions, can help you recognize your progress and stay motivated.

Take a moment to reflect on your own routine. What small step could you take today to maintain consistency? It might be a ten-minute walk, a few minutes of stretching, or another activity that helps you stay active.

Consistency does not require perfect conditions. It simply requires a willingness to continue. By approaching exercise with patience and flexibility, it becomes easier to overcome obstacles and develop a lasting commitment to physical activity.

Activities for A Healthy Lifestyle

Engaging in physical activity is one of the most direct ways to strengthen the connection between the mind and the body. When you move your body, you are not only supporting your physical health but also creating space for mental clarity, emotional balance, and resilience. Exercise has the potential to improve how you feel both physically and mentally, making it an important component of a healthy lifestyle.

Fortunately, staying active does not require a single type of exercise. There are many ways to incorporate movement into your routine, and the best activity is often the one you enjoy and feel motivated to continue.

Physical activities generally fall into several broad categories:

Aerobic activities, which increase heart rate and improve cardiovascular health. Examples include walking, running, cycling, swimming, rowing, and hiking.

Strength-based activities, which help build muscle and support endurance. These may include resistance training, weightlifting, bodyweight exercises, or structured programs such as CrossFit.

Mind–body activities, which combine physical movement with attention to breathing and mental focus. Practices such as yoga, Pilates, and Tai Chi can support both physical flexibility and mental relaxation.

Recreational and social activities, which combine exercise with enjoyment and social connection. These may include dancing, team sports, martial arts, tennis, or group fitness classes.

Choosing an activity that feels enjoyable or energizing can make it easier to maintain consistency. Rather than forcing yourself into a routine that feels unpleasant, consider exploring different forms of movement until you discover what works best for your body, your schedule, and your interests. Once you find an activity you enjoy, you can create a flexible routine that allows movement to become a natural part of your day.

Beyond the physical benefits, exercise also influences important processes within the body that affect mental well-being. Physical activity can stimulate the release of neurotransmitters such as endorphins and dopamine, which are associated with improved mood and feelings of well-being. Exercise also plays a role in regulating cortisol, a hormone involved in the body's stress response.

During physical activity, cortisol levels temporarily increase as the body adapts to the physical demands of exercise. Over time, however, regular training can help regulate cortisol levels more effectively, allowing the body to respond to stress in a more balanced way. This process helps strengthen resilience and can support improved stress management in daily life (Athanasiou, Bogdanis, & Mastorakos, 2023).

Movement can also activate multiple regions of the brain involved in emotional regulation and coordination. Activities that combine rhythm and movement, such as dancing, may further stimulate communication between the brain and other body systems. Research suggests that physical activity can influence the relationship between the nervous system and the gastrointestinal system, supporting overall health and well-being through the interconnected nature of the body (Levinthal & Strick, 2020).

To understand how this may play out in daily life, consider a common experience. Imagine you are managing multiple responsibilities at work and beginning to feel overwhelmed by deadlines. Engaging in regular physical activity, such as going for a walk, attending a fitness class, or participating in a recreational sport, can help regulate stress responses over time. As the body adapts to regular movement, it becomes better equipped to manage physical and emotional stress, allowing you to remain more focused and balanced during demanding situations.

By incorporating physical activity into your routine, you are not only strengthening your body but also supporting the systems that help your mind adapt to stress and maintain emotional well-being.

Exercise as an Investment in Yourself

Many people view exercise as another responsibility on an already busy list of obligations. Between work, family commitments, and daily responsibilities, it can sometimes feel difficult to justify setting aside time for physical activity. However, exercise is not simply another task—it is an investment in your overall well-being.

When you choose to move your body, you are supporting not only your physical health but also your emotional and mental resilience. Regular physical activity can improve energy levels, support better sleep, reduce stress, and enhance your ability to manage daily challenges. Over time, these benefits extend far beyond the moments spent exercising.

Viewing exercise as an investment can help shift your perspective. Just as you might invest time in education, relationships, or personal development, dedicating time to physical activity contributes to your long-term health and quality of life. Each workout, walk, stretch, or movement session becomes a way of supporting your future self.

This perspective also encourages self-compassion. Some days you may have more energy and motivation than others, and that is normal. What matters is recognizing that every effort, no matter how small, contributes to maintaining your health and well-being.

By approaching exercise as an act of care for yourself, it becomes easier to prioritize movement as part of your life. Over time, these choices build a foundation for a healthier, more balanced lifestyle.

Takeaway

Exercise is not simply a luxury or optional activity; it is an essential component of maintaining both physical and mental well-being. In today's increasingly sedentary world, it is important to recognize the role that regular movement plays in supporting overall health. Even dedicating about 30 minutes a day to physical activity can make a meaningful difference. Starting with manageable amounts of exercise and gradually increasing activity over time can help build a sustainable and healthy routine.

Many people face common obstacles to maintaining an active lifestyle, such as limited time, low motivation, or unrealistic expectations about what exercise should look like. Overcoming these challenges often begins with shifting your mindset and focusing on consistency rather than perfection. Small, regular efforts, whether it is a walk, a stretch, or a structured workout, can lead to lasting improvements in both physical and mental health.

Exercise also represents an investment in yourself. When you engage in physical activity, you strengthen the connection between your mind and body while supporting your energy, resilience, and overall quality of life. Exploring a variety of activities, such as walking, running, cycling, yoga, dancing, martial arts, or team sports, can help you discover forms of movement that you genuinely enjoy.

Keeping track of your activity and reflecting on your motivation can further support your progress and maintain accountability. By prioritizing movement and approaching exercise with flexibility and self-compassion, you create a foundation for a healthier and more balanced lifestyle. Over time, these choices can empower you to maintain an active life that supports both your present well-being and your future health.

Chapter 4

Finding Inner Peace with Relaxation

Chapter Four

Finding Inner Peace with Relaxation

Before we delve into the chapter on relaxation, take a deep breath in... and breathe out. Perfect. Let's begin.

The fourth element in this guide to well-being is the practice of relaxation. I use this term to describe the act of intentionally creating time for yourself and allowing your mind and body to enter a state of calm and tranquility. Experiencing moments of relaxation can bring numerous benefits to both your mental and physical well-being. It allows you to slow down the pace of life and create a pause within your day to reconnect with yourself.

Through mindful breathing and the release of physical tension, relaxation can help you feel rejuvenated, as if you are beginning again from a place of inner balance and clarity.

The following questions may help you reflect on whether you could benefit from dedicating more time to relaxation:

1. Do you often feel overwhelmed by your responsibilities?

2. Do you frequently notice tension in your muscles?
3. Do you become easily irritated or impatient?
4. Do you sometimes feel so exhausted that you think about quitting a project or job?

If you answered "yes" to any of these questions, you may benefit from intentionally creating time to relax. Taking a break does not mean you are being lazy; it means you are taking care of yourself.

Living In Stress Mode

Think about the last time you experienced significant stress. You may recall feeling your heart race, your palms become sweaty, or tension building in your shoulders or neck. These physical reactions are part of the body's natural stress response.

When the brain perceives a potential threat, it releases chemicals that prepare the body to face the challenge. This response can be helpful in short-term situations that require quick action. However, when stress becomes constant or prolonged, it can begin to negatively affect overall health (van Kraaij et al., 2020).

Chronic stress can influence many systems in the body, including heart rate, blood pressure, sleep, and concentration. Research using wearable technology has shown that ongoing stress can affect heart rate patterns throughout the day, highlighting how persistent pressure can influence the body's normal rhythms (van Kraaij et al., 2020).

Imagine constantly balancing work responsibilities, financial concerns, and personal obligations. In this situation, the brain may interpret these ongoing pressures as signals to remain alert. As a result, the body continues operating in a heightened state of tension. Over time, muscles remain tight, concentration becomes more difficult, and emotional patience may decrease.

Long-term stress can also influence how individuals regulate emotions. Research suggests that early life stress may affect emotional regulation and cognitive flexibility later in adulthood (Kalia & Knauft, 2020). However, learning healthy coping strategies—such as cognitive reappraisal, which involves reframing difficult situations in a more constructive way—can help reduce emotional strain and improve resilience.

Suppressing emotions, on the other hand, can sometimes intensify stress. Allowing yourself to process emotions through healthy outlets—such as conversation, writing, meditation, or creative expression—can support emotional balance.

Stress is not meant to disappear entirely from life. Instead, it exists as part of the natural rhythm of being human. The goal is not to eliminate stress but to learn how to move between moments of pressure and moments of calm.

The Power of Relaxation

Relaxation is the body's natural counterbalance to stress. When you intentionally slow your breathing and allow your muscles to release tension, your nervous system shifts toward a calmer state.

Relaxation techniques signal to the brain that the environment is safe, allowing the body to move out of a state of constant alertness. Over time, practicing relaxation regularly can help train the nervous system to return to calm more easily.

In my therapeutic work with clients, I often incorporate a brief breathing exercise at the end of sessions. This practice allows individuals to release any emotional tension that may have surfaced during therapy.

Many clients report leaving the session feeling lighter, calmer, and more centered before returning to their daily responsibilities.

Research has also shown that relaxation practices can influence biological processes in the body. Studies examining gene expression before and after relaxation exercises found changes related to energy metabolism and stress regulation (Bhasin et al., 2013). These findings suggest that relaxation may contribute to improved cellular functioning and overall health.

By regularly practicing relaxation techniques, you give your mind and body an opportunity to reset. Instead of beginning each day immediately engaging with technology or stressors, you can take a few moments to breathe, observe your surroundings, and approach the day with greater intention.

Listening to Your Body's Signals

Many people move through their daily routines without fully noticing the signals their body sends when it needs rest. Stress does not always appear as obvious anxiety or emotional distress. Often, it manifests through physical sensations such as headaches, fatigue, muscle tightness, irritability, or difficulty concentrating.

Because modern culture often emphasizes productivity and constant activity, individuals may learn to ignore these signals and push through exhaustion. Over time, this pattern can lead to chronic tension and emotional burnout.

Learning to listen to your body's signals is an important step toward improving your well-being. When you begin to notice how stress affects your body, you can respond earlier rather than waiting until tension becomes overwhelming.

By recognizing these cues, relaxation becomes more than an occasional activity—it becomes a preventive practice that helps maintain emotional and physical balance.

Activities for Relaxation

There are many activities that can help promote relaxation and restore a sense of calm. Exploring different approaches can help you discover the ones that best fit your preferences and lifestyle.

Aromatherapy

Aromatherapy involves using essential oils through inhalation or topical application. Certain scents, such as lavender or citrus oils, have been associated with reduced stress and improved mood (Freeman et al., 2019). Some research has also shown that combining aromatherapy with calming music may help reduce anxiety levels (Son et al., 2019).

Massage Therapy

Receiving a massage on your back or shoulders is widely recognized as a deeply relaxing experience. Massage therapy can provide benefits not only for individuals but also for couples, benefiting them emotionally and physically. In a research study, a short educational massage program called Positive Massage (PM) was evaluated for healthy but stressed couples. The study aimed to determine the immediate and lasting effects of the program on well-being, perceived stress and coping, and relationship satisfaction among couples. The results showed that the PM program had a significant positive impact on couples' mental well-being, perceived stress, and coping (Naruse & Moss, 2019). When individuals are in a state of relaxation, they typically exhibit lower blood pressure levels and experience less tension throughout their bodies. Consequently, massage therapy serves as an effective means to reduce stress and tension. Integrating regular massages into your weekly or monthly routine can be an excellent strategy for promoting overall well-being and enhancing your ability to manage stress effectively.

Breathing Exercises

Breathing exercises are a valuable tool that can empower you to regulate your breath and unlock numerous health benefits for your body and mind. In a study conducted in 2017, researchers set out to examine the impact of diaphragmatic (or abdominal) breathing on stress levels, negative emotions, and attention. Over the course of eight weeks, a group of 20 participants received 20 breathing sessions. The results revealed notable improvements in attention, a reduction in negative emotions, and lower levels of cortisol, the stress hormone (Ma et al., 2017). By incorporating regular practice of breathing exercises into your daily routine, you can invite these benefits into your own life. This includes the practice of Progressive Muscle Relaxation, where you need to tense for a few seconds each muscle of your body and then relax it (Tee et al., 2022). In order to stay relaxed during this technique, it is essential to practice deep breathing. Imagine starting your day with a few minutes of deep breathing, allowing your body to oxygenate and your mind to find a sense of calm.

By repeating this routine over time, you may begin to notice subtle yet powerful shifts in your well-being.

Whether you are going through a stressful workday, facing challenging emotions, or simply seeking a moment of tranquility, the practice of breathing exercises offers a sanctuary of calm within reach. In the last section of this chapter, you will discover detailed instructions on how to engage in diaphragmatic or abdominal breathing. Through consistent practice of these techniques, you can harness their transformative potential to enhance your overall well-being and effectively manage stress.

Creating a Calming Environment

Creating a calming environment at home can play an important role in supporting relaxation and emotional well-being. In today's fast-paced world, having a designated space where you can pause, breathe, and recharge can make a meaningful difference in how you manage daily stress. This space does not need to be large or elaborate; even a small corner of your home can become a peaceful place dedicated to relaxation.

The goal is to create an environment that encourages you to slow down and disconnect from daily pressures. The following suggestions can help you design a space that promotes calmness and comfort.

Choose a Comfortable Location

Begin by selecting a location where you naturally feel at ease. This could be a bedroom, a quiet corner of your living room, a reading chair near a window, or any space that allows you to disconnect from distractions. If you do not already have a specific area for relaxation, consider transforming a small part of your home into one.

Natural light can also enhance the calming atmosphere. Sitting near a window where you can see trees, the sky, or outdoor scenery can contribute to a sense of tranquility and connection with nature.

Minimize Distractions and Maintain Organization

A cluttered environment can sometimes contribute to feelings of stress or mental overload. Try to keep your relaxation space clean and organized so that it feels inviting rather than overwhelming.

If possible, avoid having televisions or other distractions in this area. This space is meant to support quiet reflection and rest. Simple organization strategies, such as keeping surfaces tidy and limiting unnecessary objects, can help maintain a peaceful atmosphere.

Personalize the Space with Meaningful Elements

Adding items that bring you comfort or positive emotions can make your relaxation space feel more personal and inviting. Soft textures such as blankets, cushions, or a comfortable chair can encourage physical relaxation.

Some people enjoy incorporating objects that hold personal meaning, such as photographs, inspirational quotes, small plants, candles, or decorative items that evoke a sense of calm. In my therapy office, I have a small relaxation area with a diffuser, a sound bowl, and a tabletop water fountain. These elements help create a tranquil environment where clients can practice breathing techniques and mindfulness exercises.

Adjust Lighting for a Soothing Atmosphere

Lighting has a powerful influence on mood. Soft, warm lighting can help create a relaxing atmosphere that encourages the body to slow down. Lamps with adjustable brightness, dim lighting, or candles can help establish a peaceful environment. Natural light during the daytime can also be beneficial. Opening curtains or sitting near a window can bring a sense of openness and calm to the space.

Incorporate Calming Scents

Scent can have a strong connection to emotions and memory. Using gentle aromas such as lavender, chamomile, sandalwood, or citrus can contribute to a soothing environment.

You might use an essential oil diffuser, scented candles, or incense to introduce calming scents into your space. It is important to choose fragrances that you personally find relaxing and to avoid any scents that may trigger allergies or discomfort.

Engaging your senses—through touch, scent, sight, and sound—can help bring your attention fully into the present moment. When your senses are gently stimulated, your mind is less likely to wander toward worries about the past or future. Instead, you can focus on the experience of relaxation itself.

Simple Everyday Relaxation Activities

Relaxation does not always require structured techniques. Many everyday activities can also help reduce stress and restore emotional balance.

Reading a book, spending time in nature, gardening, painting, practicing yoga, or listening to music can all serve as effective ways to unwind. Engaging in hobbies allows your mind to shift away from constant problem-solving and responsibilities.

Some individuals also enjoy creating a relaxing ritual at home, such as taking a warm bath, lighting candles, playing calming music, or preparing a cup of herbal tea. These simple moments of intentional rest can provide a meaningful pause within a busy day.

The goal is not to perform relaxation perfectly but to create moments throughout your routine where you allow your mind and body to slow down.

Practice: Breathing Techniques for Relaxation

Progressive Muscle Relaxation

The main goal of the progressive muscle relaxation technique is to decrease the tension in your muscles and decrease levels of stress and anxiety. Many individuals have become used to a constant state of tension, often overlooking, or disregarding the pain in their muscles as they carry on with their daily activities. They may experience pain in areas such as the back, neck, shoulders, or even the jaw from clenching their teeth.

Practicing progressive muscle relaxation allows you to relax each and cultivate a habit of promoting relaxation in your mind and body on a regular basis instead of automatically being tense. To apply this method, begin by lying down on a comfortable surface or sitting in a relaxed chair position. You can then initiate a systematic and rhythmic process of alternating between tensing and releasing various muscle groups in your body (Tee et al., 2022). You can do this technique with your eyes closed or opened. Make sure you take deep breaths in between to stay relaxed.

Extended periods of sitting at a desk or prolonged standing due to work can lead to muscle discomfort and strain. These physical discomforts can impact individuals' well-being and hinder their productivity. Fortunately, integrating progressive muscle relaxation into their daily routine offers a solution. By consciously and systematically relaxing each muscle group, individuals can gradually alleviate the accumulated tension and discomfort. Through this practice, they can relax, alleviate physical strain, and restore a sense of balance to their body.

Diaphragmatic or Abdominal Breathing

This simple yet powerful practice offers numerous benefits, including the ability to slow down your heart rate and stabilize your blood pressure (Ma et al., 2017). As a result, you can achieve a profound sense of calm and tranquility. By practicing this technique, you will experience the expansion of your abdomen during inhalation and its contraction during exhalation (Ma et al., 2017). To help you remain calm during the breathing technique, try to envision yourself moving in slow motion. This way your brain can develop a sense of tranquility, preventing any tendency for rapid or abrupt movements that might disrupt the calming effect. To begin practicing diaphragmatic breathing, follow these steps:

1. Sit in a comfortable position or lie flat on your bed, or another comfortable, flat surface.

2. If you are sitting up, try to relax your shoulders.

3. You can put a hand on your chest and the other hand on your stomach.

4. Breathe in slowly through your nose while expanding your abdomen.

5. Hold your breath for 2 seconds.

6. Exhale slowly through your mouth while slowly contracting your abdomen.

7. If you experience automatic thoughts that come to your mind and disrupt your rhythm, accept them as just thoughts and let them go. You can continue focusing on your breathing and notice how your body responds to inhaling and exhaling. This is a great opportunity to practice mindfulness.

8. Repeat this exercise for at least 10 to 15 minutes.

5-4-3-2-1 Sensory Grounding Technique

This grounding technique is a simple and effective exercise designed to help individuals reconnect with the present moment by utilizing their five senses. By focusing on sensory experiences, you can shift your attention away from overwhelming emotions or thoughts, promoting a sense of calm. The 5-4-3-2-1 technique is beneficial for several reasons. First, it helps reduce anxiety by distracting you from anxious thoughts and feelings, providing immediate relief from stress. Second, it enhances mindfulness by encouraging you to stay present and engaged with your environment, which can improve overall mental well-being. Additionally, engaging with your senses can activate your body's relaxation response, reducing tension and promoting a sense of peace.

You can use the technique during moments of anxiety, before stressful events like public speaking or exams, when feeling disconnected, or as part of a daily mindfulness practice. By incorporating this grounding technique into your wellness toolkit, you can develop a practical strategy for managing stress and enhancing your mental well-being.

To practice the 5-4-3-2-1 grounding technique, follow these steps:

1. **Find a Comfortable Space**: Sit or stand in a quiet place where you can focus without distractions.

2. **Take a Deep Breath**: Begin by taking a few deep breaths to center yourself. Inhale deeply through your nose and exhale **slowly** through your mouth.

3. **Identify Your Senses:**

5 Things You Can See: Look around you and name five things you can see. It could be anything from a picture on the wall to the color of the furniture.

4 Things You Can Touch: Notice four things you can physically touch. This might include the texture of your clothing, the feeling of the chair beneath you, or the ground under your feet.

3 Things You Can Hear: Listen closely and identify three sounds. These could be the hum of a fan, birds chirping outside, or distant conversations.

2 Things You Can Smell: Take a moment to identify two scents in your environment. If you can't smell anything, think of your two favorite scents.

1 Thing You Can Taste: Focus on one thing you can taste. It might be the aftertaste of a meal, a sip of water, or simply the air in your mouth.

Guided Imagery: Your Mind's Soothing Journey

Imagine this: As you take a deep breath, you step into a world where your mind feels calm, safe, and open. In this world, the stress of your day fades away like clouds slowly drifting from a clear blue sky. Picture yourself creating a moment of peace and clarity, guiding your thoughts through a landscape of serenity.

Guided imagery is just like taking a mental journey. It can be as simple as imagining a peaceful beach, where the sound of the waves gently lapping the shore invites you to relax deeper with each breath. Or it could be a walk through a serene forest, where the crisp air and the scent of pine remind you that nature's beauty is always there to support you.

The beauty of guided imagery lies in its simplicity. You do not need anything special, just your mind and a few minutes of quiet time. Whether you are feeling overwhelmed or just need a moment to reset, this practice allows you to tap into your inner calm. You can choose a place that makes you feel completely at ease—a cozy cabin in the mountains, or a field of sunflowers bathed in golden light. Whatever it is, it is your space, and it is always waiting for you.

Why does this work? Because our minds are powerful. When we visualize peaceful, positive images, it is like giving ourselves a little break from the noise of the outside world. We allow our body to relax and our thoughts to quiet down. Guided imagery helps remind us that, no matter what is happening around us, there is always a space within where we can find stillness.

You can use this simple practice whenever you need to recharge, before bed, during a stressful moment, or even as a slow start to your day. It is a personal, loving gift to yourself, inviting balance and peace whenever you need it most. If it is difficult for you to imagine the details or stay focused, you can always use an app to guide you.

I have shared this practice with some of my clients at the end of our sessions to cope with any negative emotion that surfaced during therapy. I would play calming music in the background, they would often close their eyes, and I would guide them through what to imagine; for example, walking in the forest. What always fascinated me was that, at the end, when I would ask what they saw or how they felt, they would describe things I had not even mentioned. I believe that was their imagination fully embracing the experience. With a smile, they would share seeing a river or butterflies, and it was heartwarming to see how this simple exercise helped them, even if it was just to bring a smile or shift their thoughts to something more positive.

Practicing relaxation techniques can help you disrupt the persistent cycle of chronic stress that is often present in daily life. This uninterrupted chain of stress, which often accompanies a busy lifestyle, can take a toll on both your physical and mental well-being. By intentionally interrupting this cycle, you allow your body and mind to experience a much-needed rest from constant tension and strain.

Relaxation Practice Tracker:

Use the following template as a self-care tracker to monitor your self-care activities and ensure you prioritize relaxation:

Date: ____________

1. Rate your overall stress level on a scale of 1-10 (1 being low, 10 being high):

Stress level: ________

2. Choose at least three self-care activities from the list below that you will prioritize today:

- o Practice deep breathing exercise for 10 minutes

- o Take a relaxing bath or shower

- o Engage in a creative hobby (e.g., painting, writing, knitting)

- o Spend time in nature

- o Listen to calming music

- o Read a book or listen to an audiobook

- o Practice yoga or stretching

- o Write in a journal.

- ○ Engage in a physical activity you enjoy (e.g., walking, dancing, swimming)

3. After completing each self-care activity, rate how it made you feel on a scale of 1-5 (1 being low, 5 being high):

Activity 1: _________

Activity 2: _________

Activity 3: _________

4. Reflect on the self-care activities you engaged in today. Did they help you relax and reduce stress? Write a brief description of your experience and any insights gained:

-

____

-

____

-

____

5. Additional thoughts or reflections on your self-care practice today:

-

____

-

____

Use this self-care tracker to monitor your engagement with relaxation techniques. By consistently engaging in these activities, you can cultivate a more relaxed and balanced lifestyle.

Takeaway

Incorporating relaxation into your daily life is essential for maintaining emotional and physical well-being. By intentionally creating moments of calm, you can counteract the effects of chronic stress and support your body's natural ability to restore balance.

Relaxation can take many forms, from breathing exercises and mindfulness practices to engaging in hobbies or creating a peaceful environment at home. The key is discovering the approaches that resonate most with you and integrating them into your routine.

When relaxation becomes a regular practice rather than an occasional escape, it helps break the cycle of constant tension. Over time, these moments of pause allow you to slow down, reconnect with the present moment, and approach life with greater clarity and resilience.

True well-being is not defined solely by productivity or achievement. It also includes the ability to rest, reflect, and enjoy meaningful moments with yourself and with others.

By prioritizing relaxation, you create space for a more balanced, intentional, and fulfilling life.

Chapter 5
Cultivating Mental Well-being

Chapter Five

Cultivating Mental Well-being

The fifth element in this wellness guide is cultivating your mental well-being. This is profoundly influenced by the interconnected elements discussed in the previous chapters. To improve your mental well-being it is important to prioritize sleep, nutrition, relaxation, and exercise.

Creating and nurturing mental well-being involves developing a positive outlook on the world and approaching situations and people with less stress and tension. However, when faced with inadequate sleep, fatigue, stress, and potential deficiencies in hydration or essential nutrients, it becomes difficult to view life with clarity, vitality, and a positive mindset.

The following questions can help you understand your mental well-being:

1. Do you sometimes struggle to remember the good and positive things you have in life?

2. Do you find it hard to identify and achieve your goals in life?

3. Are you experiencing feelings of mental burnout?

If you answered "yes" to the previous questions, this chapter contains valuable knowledge and practical techniques for you. Within these pages, you will find information and exercises designed to assist you in breaking negative patterns in your approach to life. These activities will become integral components of your wellness routine, offering ongoing benefits.

The Power of Mental Well-being

In my role as a mental health therapist, I frequently discuss with my clients the practices they engage in at home to enhance their mental well-being. These practices play a vital role in improving the therapeutic experience and working towards their goal of recovery. As mentioned before, your daily habits have a profound impact on your day-to-day life and overall lifestyle.

Many people experience periods when negative thoughts start to dominate their mindset. For example, someone might frequently compare themselves to others at work and begin to feel that they are not successful enough. Over time, repeated self-criticism can lead to feelings of frustration, discouragement, or inadequacy. When these thoughts become habitual, they can influence how a person views themselves, their abilities, and their future.

There is a growing understanding that the mental well-being of employees plays a vital role in their overall well-being. Poor mental well-being and workplace stressors can contribute to various physical ailments, including hypertension, cardiovascular conditions and diabetes, among other problems (Rajgopal, 2010). Poor mental well-being can also affect employers and businesses. This includes increased absenteeism, decreased productivity, and profits. It can also lead to employee burnout, severely impacting their ability to contribute meaningfully to both personal and professional aspects of their lives (Rajgopal, 2010).

Contrary to common belief, well-being is not achieved through wealth or power only (Cloninger, 2006). Well-being can be attained through the development of one's character, which fosters self-awareness and ultimately leads to greater happiness (Cloninger, 2006). By focusing on personal growth and introspection, individuals can attain a deeper sense of well-being and find lasting contentment.

Understanding Your Thought Patterns

Before exploring specific practices that support mental well-being, it is helpful to understand the powerful role that thoughts play in shaping emotional experiences.

Our thoughts influence how we interpret situations, how we respond emotionally, and how we behave. Two people can experience the same situation but interpret it very differently depending on their thought patterns. One person may view a challenge as an opportunity for growth, while another may perceive it as evidence of failure or inadequacy.

Over time, repeated thought patterns can become automatic. Individuals may develop habits of worrying, self-criticism, or focusing primarily on negative outcomes. When these patterns persist, they can contribute to increased stress, anxiety, or feelings of discouragement.

The good news is that thought patterns can be changed. By developing awareness of how the mind operates and intentionally practicing healthier mental habits, individuals can gradually reshape their thinking.

The strategies discussed in the following sections are designed to help cultivate more balanced and supportive thought patterns that contribute to improved mental well-being.

Practices for Cultivating Mental Well-being

There are several practices that can help individuals strengthen mental well-being and create more positive emotional experiences. These practices encourage reflection, self-awareness, and intentional thinking patterns that promote resilience and psychological balance.

Some of the most effective practices include cultivating gratitude, using positive reminders and affirmations, practicing mindfulness, and engaging in reflective journaling.

Gratitude

The American Psychological Association defines gratitude as a sense of appreciation and joy when individuals recognize the positive aspects of their lives (American Psychological Association, n.d.). You can cultivate gratitude for even the simplest things, like enjoying a sunny day. There are various ways to incorporate gratitude into your life, such as writing gratitude letters to yourself or others, expressing thanks through thoughtful notes, and integrating gratitude into your relaxation routine. Practicing gratitude can help bring positive thoughts into your mind, creating a sense of positivity. This practice has been found to increase social desirability and decrease loneliness (Caputo, 2015).

In an effort to explore the potential benefits of gratitude in promoting well-being, a group of researchers conducted a randomized clinical trial (a type of research study where participants are randomly assigned to different groups to ensure fairness and reduce bias in the study) to investigate the impact of a gratitude intervention on the well-being and mental health of adults. This research study involved 1,337 participants, consisting of one intervention group they called "gratitude group" with 446 participants and two control groups called "hassles group" with 444 participants and "neutral events group" with 447 participants (Cunha, Pellanda, and Reppold, 2019).

The participants within the intervention group were instructed to write daily gratitude lists for 14 consecutive days, documenting moments for which they felt grateful during each day. The participants within the control groups were instructed to think about and write down five experiences they had to deal with that were annoying or affected them. The outcomes the researchers wanted to assess were depression, happiness, life satisfaction, and affect (reference). To assess those outcomes, the participants completed three different questionnaires before the intervention, right after the intervention, and again 14 days after they completed the intervention. The questionnaires included the Positive Affect and Negative Affect Schedule (PANAS), the Subjective Happiness Scale (SHS), and the Center for Epidemiological Studies Depression Scale (CES-D). Due to the dropout of some participants, the final number of participants was 410 (Cunha, Pellanda, and Reppold, 2019).

Prior to the intervention, there were no significant differences among the groups in any of the examined variables. After completing the gratitude intervention, researchers found an increase in positive affect, subjective happiness, and life satisfaction, as well as a decrease in negative affect and symptoms of depression. The magnitude of these changes in positive affect was greater in the gratitude intervention group compared to the control groups (Cunha, Pellanda, and Reppold, 2019).

Additionally, a team of researchers used brain scanning techniques called neuroimaging or MRI to investigate the connection between gratitude, altruism, and behavioral responses to charitable actions. They wanted to see if self-reported feelings of gratitude were related to self-reported measures of altruism and how the brain responded when observing money being given to charity or oneself. The goal was to determine if gratitude could be seen as a moral and expressive emotion that influences our brain's reward system. To test this, participants were randomly assigned to either keep a gratitude journal or a control journal for three weeks. Before and after the study, their brain activity related to altruism was measured (Karns, Moore, and Mayr, 2017).

The study involved 33 female participants aged 18-35 who were not taking certain medications, had no neurological or psychiatric conditions, and were willing to participate in a journaling study. The results showed that gratitude was associated with increased altruism. Specifically, after three weeks of journaling, participants in the gratitude group showed stronger brain activity in the ventromedial prefrontal cortex (VMPFC) when observing altruistic money transfers, compared to those in the control group. The VMPFC is a region in the brain that is sensitive to the value and context of rewards. This suggests that engaging in gratitude practices can influence our brain's response to acts of altruism. Overall, this study demonstrates that interventions targeting prosocial and moral emotions, like gratitude, can lead to changes in neural activity that reflect genuine concern for others (Karns, Moore, and Mayr, 2017).

In conclusion, based on the findings of researcher studies, there is evidence of the effectiveness of practicing gratitude in promoting positive emotional well-being and overall life satisfaction. When individuals actively engage in gratitude, their mindset shifts towards a more positive and appreciative outlook. It redirects their attention to the blessings and positive aspects of their lives and the result is a sense of overall life satisfaction.

Gratitude Journal Exercise

One way to develop a gratitude practice is by keeping a simple gratitude journal. At the end of each day, write down three things you are grateful for. These do not need to be major events. Small experiences, such as a supportive conversation, a pleasant walk, or a moment of relaxation, can also be meaningful.

Over time, this practice helps train the mind to notice positive experiences more readily, which can contribute to improved emotional well-being.

Date: _____________

1. List five things you are grateful for today:

   • ________________________________

   • ________________________________

   • ________________________________

   • ________________________________

   • ________________________________

2. Reflect on why you are grateful for each item on your list. Write a brief explanation or description for each:

   • ________________________________

   • ________________________________

   • ________________________________

   • ________________________________

   • ________________________________

3. How did focusing on gratitude today make you feel? Describe any positive emotions or changes in perspective you experienced:

   • ________________________________

   • ________________________________

   • ________________________________

4. Did you notice any effects on your overall well-being or outlook throughout the day? If so, describe how gratitude impacted your mood, mindset, or interactions with others:

- _____________________________________
- _____________________________________
- _____________________________________

5. Additional thoughts or reflections:

- _____________________________________
- _____________________________________
- _____________________________________

Positive Reminders: The Power of Words

The words we hear and the words we say to ourselves can significantly influence how we feel and how we perform in various situations. Language has the ability to shape perceptions, affect motivation, and even alter physical experiences. This has been demonstrated by studies exploring the connection between spoken words and pain processing in the brain.

Research has shown that the specific words used prior to and during painful medical procedures can significantly impact the level of discomfort experienced by individuals. For instance, words associated with negative emotions or pain can trigger stronger activation in key brain regions involved in pain perception, including the anterior cingulate cortex and the somatosensory cortex, compared to neutral words (Ritter et al., 2019).

The study utilized functional magnetic resonance imaging (fMRI) to analyze participants' reactions to painful stimuli that were preceded by various types of words. The results demonstrated that pain-related words not only increased the perceived intensity of pain but also activated brain areas associated with sensory and motor responses. This indicates that the brain's response to language can physically intensify the sensation of pain, underscoring the profound connection between language and our bodily experiences (Ritter et al., 2019).

The implications of this go beyond just pain management; they highlight the power of words to influence not only emotional states but also physical experiences. Thus, choosing positive, soothing words could help in medical, therapeutic, and everyday settings to create a healthier mental and physical response.

By understanding how words can influence the brain for pain or relief, we can see the importance of fostering positive language, especially in situations of stress, discomfort, or uncertainty, as it can have real consequences for both mental and physical health.

Another study examined how verbal encouragement from physical education teachers influenced students' physical and emotional responses during small-sided soccer games. Sixteen male students participated in sessions with verbal encouragement and others without. The results indicated that sessions with verbal encouragement led to significantly higher perceived effort, and enjoyment, along with improved mood and reduced tension compared to those without encouragement. These findings underline the positive impact of verbal encouragement on students' motivation and engagement in physical activities, demonstrating its crucial role in enhancing their overall experience (Sahli et al., 2020).

Moreover, the benefits of verbal encouragement extend beyond the realm of physical education. In various life situations, positive words and support can motivate individuals to overcome challenges, build self-esteem, and foster resilience. This encouragement not only enhances performance in sports but also in academics, career pursuits, and personal growth. By promoting a supportive environment, verbal encouragement can empower individuals to strive for their goals, improve their mental well-being, and cultivate a more positive outlook on life.

In addition to external support, practicing self-affirmations can have a powerful effect on your mental and emotional well-being. Self-affirmations can have a powerful effect on your mental and emotional well-being by boosting self-compassion. When you affirm personal values, it not only strengthens your self-image but also helps you treat yourself with more kindness and understanding. This increase in self-compassion can inspire more positive behaviors, including greater empathy toward others. The process of acknowledging your worth through self-affirmation allows for a shift in focus from self-criticism to self-acceptance, which can improve your overall mood and emotional resilience (Lindsay & Creswell, 2014).

Practice Self-affirmations:

1. Start by identifying a core value you hold dear, such as kindness, perseverance, or creativity.

2. Create a simple affirmation based on that value, such as, "I am resilient and can handle life's challenges with strength and grace."

3. Write it down or say this affirmation to yourself each morning or when facing difficulties.

Reflecting on this value can help shift your mindset toward self-compassion, allowing you to respond to challenges with patience and empathy, fostering both personal growth and emotional well-being.

Mindfulness

Mindfulness is the practice of intentionally focusing attention on the present moment with openness and without judgment. Rather than dwelling on the past or worrying about the future, mindfulness encourages individuals to fully experience what is happening in the present.

What this means is that when individuals practice mindfulness, they have the ability to observe their thoughts and emotions without getting carried away by them. They become more attuned to the sensations in their body, the quality of their breath, and the subtle nuances of their surroundings. This heightened awareness allows them to fully experience the present moment without being preoccupied by regrets of the past or anxieties about the future. This awareness can be accomplished by the practice of meditation or any other common activities of daily living where you fully focus on what you are doing, such as eating, walking, cooking, and driving.

For example, imagine a person sitting in a park, practicing mindfulness. They focus their attention on the sensation of the grass beneath their feet, the warmth of the sunlight on their skin, and the gentle rustling of leaves in the wind. They notice the thoughts and emotions that arise, such as worries or distractions, but instead of getting lost in them, they acknowledge them with kindness and let them pass without judgment. In this state of mindfulness, they are fully present, savoring the beauty of the moment and finding peace within themselves.

Research studies have provided evidence that incorporating mindfulness into treatments can effectively decrease feelings of anxiety and depression. Moreover, mindfulness practices have demonstrated potential in reducing blood pressure levels, enhancing sleep quality, and assisting individuals in managing pain (National Institute of Mental Health, June 2021). One powerful technique to ground oneself in the present moment, particularly when the mind is filled with numerous thoughts, is to gently interrupt the stream of thinking and redirect the focus to the present experience.

This can be achieved by doing a body scan where you begin by taking a series of deep breaths, allowing yourself to become grounded in the present moment.

Direct your attention towards your feet and observe how they feel. Gradually, shift your awareness upwards, scanning your body from your legs to your stomach, arms, hands, neck, and finally, your head.

Pay attention to any sensations or discomfort that arise, without attempting to alter or evaluate them. Engaging in regular body scans can facilitate the cultivation of mindfulness (National Institute of Mental Health, June 2021). Incorporating regular body scans into your mindfulness practice can help foster a deeper connection with the present moment and enhance overall mindfulness.

Some people instinctively tend to wake up and immediately remember their tasks and responsibilities, which might have become an automatic task. Often, thinking about these responsibilities can cause stress and worry, and this mindset can overshadow the beauty of a new day and the opportunity to experience the present moment. This habit of starting the day with negative thoughts can set a negative tone for the rest of the day. While it may be seen as a way to remember tasks, it can also have a negative impact on the beginning of the day.

Many of my clients have mentioned this issue in therapy. To counteract this pattern, I frequently recommend taking a few minutes to acknowledge the fact that you just woke up. Look around and try to find something in your room to appreciate. This practice is simple, it can last a few minutes, but it is a valuable habit to adopt. By taking this pause before engaging in worry or stress, you become more aware of the present moment and recognize the precious gift of life. Simply, look around the room while you are waking up and acknowledge it is a new day. These first thoughts will ground you and help you set the day in a mindful way.

Journaling

Practicing journaling can be another powerful and transformative experience that can bring happiness and liberation to your life. In therapy, I often convey to my clients that documenting their thoughts, emotions, and personal experiences can empower them to explore their emotions, develop deep self-awareness, and discover a profound sense of liberation.

A journaling technique called Positive Affect Journaling (PAJ) is a powerful method that involves writing about positive aspects of oneself and life. In one study, participants who engaged in structured emotional writing sessions over a period of several weeks reported improvements in mental well-being, reduced distress, and enhanced resilience (Smyth et al., 2018).

One way to put the PAJ technique into practice is by setting aside dedicated time each day to write about positive aspects of yourself and your life. Start by reflecting on your day and identifying moments or experiences that brought you joy, gratitude, or a sense of accomplishment. Write about these positive experiences in detail, describing the emotions and sensations associated with them. Focus on the positive aspects and the impact they had on your well-being. For example, you could write about a personal achievement you are proud of, or a moment of connection with a loved one. By consistently engaging in this practice, you can enhance your awareness of positive experiences and cultivate a more positive mindset overall.

On the other hand, if you often find yourself dwelling on the negatives, frequently complaining, or feeling anxious about upcoming events, take a moment to reflect on your daily routine, from morning to night. Consider what might be triggering these negative thought patterns. By examining your habits and experiences, you may discover the source of your negative mindset. Journaling can be a helpful tool for this, writing down what typically causes your negative thoughts allows you to confront them openly, instead of letting them linger in your mind. Is it the fear of failure? Is it the reminder of a previous event? Once they are on paper, you can start taking steps to address them or begin shifting how you perceive them.

Journaling can be a great opportunity to observe your thoughts, reflect on different aspects of your life, and gain insights into your well-being. You can use the following prompts as a guide during your journaling practice to delve deeper into your thoughts and emotions (Cloninger, 2006).

Journaling Prompts

1. What things or people make me happy?

   Reflect on the activities, experiences, or moments that bring you joy and happiness. Consider the people, places, or things that contribute to your sense of well-being.

2. What contributes to feelings of unhappiness in my life?

   Explore the factors that contribute to feelings of unhappiness or dissatisfaction in your life. Identify any negative thought patterns or external influences that may impact your well-being.

3. What things contribute to my well-being?

    Reflect on the times when you have felt a sense of peace and tranquility. Consider the strategies or practices that help calm your mind and bring about a state of well-being.

4. Finding purpose in life

    Contemplate the deeper aspects of your life and explore what gives it meaning and purpose. Reflect on your values, beliefs, and spiritual experiences that contribute to a sense of fulfillment.

(Cloninger, 2006)

Enhancing Well-being Through Personal Growth

Mental well-being is not only influenced by daily habits but also by the sense of purpose and direction individuals experience in their lives. Personal growth involves exploring goals, identifying meaningful values, and making choices that align with those values.

When individuals pursue goals that reflect their personal interests and values, they often experience greater motivation and fulfillment.

Setting Life Goals

Imagine you are a hiker embarking on a challenging hiking trail. Without a clear goal or destination in mind, you wander without purpose through the wilderness. You may take detours, lose your way, and become disoriented. Your journey lacks direction and intention, and you may feel a sense of aimlessness and lack of motivation.

Now, picture a different scenario. You have a specific landmark in mind that you would like to reach. You study the trail map, equip yourself with the necessary gear, and set off on your journey with a determined mindset. Along the way, you encounter difficult paths, unexpected obstacles, and unpredictable weather conditions. However, with your goal in sight, you stay focused, motivated, and resilient. As you make progress towards your desired destination, you experience a sense of accomplishment, fulfillment, and renewed energy.

In both scenarios, the difference lies in having a clear goal. Without it, you may wander through life without purpose, feeling lost and uninspired. But when you set specific goals, whether it is reaching a mountain peak or achieving your personal aspirations, you create a roadmap that fuels your motivation and discipline to move towards success.

As a mental health therapist, I had the honor of witnessing the transformative power of goal setting in the lives of my clients. One particular client was dealing with low self-esteem and a lack of clear purpose. Throughout our therapy sessions, we worked collaboratively to explore his passions, values, and long-term aspirations. With newfound clarity, he set a remarkable goal: to establish his own company. Over the course of our sessions, I observed his determination as he crafted a comprehensive business plan, actively sought funding opportunities, and diligently networked with potential partners. Despite encountering numerous obstacles along the way, his commitment to his goal kept him focused and motivated. He gained more confidence, self-belief, and overall mental well-being. Witnessing his progress was inspiring.

Take a moment to reflect on your current life and the daily routines that shape your days, whether it is work, home, or other regular activities. In the midst of these routines, your mind overflows with aspirations and dreams, longing for a happier and more fulfilling existence. Often, these desires remain distant and unattainable, lingering as mere thoughts. But what if you take a break from the routine and invest a moment to write down your most significant aspirations or goals?

By doing so, you create a list of realistic goals, each with a roadmap of actions and achievable timeframes. This process brings forth a newfound clarity, as your path to success unfolds before you. With focused determination and discipline, your daily choices and actions become aligned with your primary objective. As you conquer each milestone with a sense of accomplishment, a deep sense of fulfillment ignites within, motivating you to embrace the next goal on your journey.

Life Goals Chart

1. Specific Goal: ______________________________

    - Steps/Actions:

        ○

        ○

        ○

    - Motivation: *(What inspires me to work towards this goal? Why is this goal important to me?)*

2. Specific Goal: ______________________________

    - Steps/Actions:

        ○

        ○

        ○

    - Motivation: *(What inspires me to work towards this goal? Why is this goal important to me?)*

3. Specific Goal: ______________________________

    - Steps/Actions:

        ○

        ○

○

- Motivation: *(What inspires me to work towards this goal? Why is this goal important to me?)*

Note: Feel free to add more goals and steps as needed. Remember to review and update your goals regularly to track your progress and make adjustments accordingly.

Finding Your Value

The concept of personal values plays a crucial role in shaping people's lives and guiding their actions. It encompasses a rich and diverse composition of beliefs and principles that influence their decisions, behaviors, and sense of purpose. Understanding and clarifying your personal values is fundamental to setting meaningful goals and effectively navigating the complexities of life. By delving into the diverse nature of personal values, you can gain insight into their various dimensions and the significant impact they have on different aspects of your life (Gamage, Dehideniya, & Ekanayake, 2021).

For example, someone who strongly values creativity may feel limited in a role that offers little opportunity for innovation. Similarly, a person who values helping others may feel more fulfilled in activities that involve mentoring, teaching, or community involvement.

Identifying your personal values is crucial for self-esteem and personal growth as it provides a clear understanding of what truly matters to you. When you are aware of your values, you can align your actions and decisions with them, which leads to a sense of authenticity and fulfillment. Every person has their unique value and worth in this world. Finding your value as a person is a journey that begins with self-discovery and acceptance.

It is about recognizing and embracing your strengths, talents, and passions. You are capable of amazing things, and your value is not determined by your job, relationship status, or social standing. Your value is inherent in who you are as a person. Take the time to reflect on your positive qualities and achievements, and do not forget to be kind to yourself along the way. Remember, you are worthy of love, respect, and happiness just the way you are.

According to the Values in Action (VIA) Classification of Strengths project by Nansook Park and Christopher Peterson (2009), there are 24 widely valued strengths (Park & Peterson 2009):

<table>
<tr><td>Religiousness</td><td>Teamwork</td></tr>
<tr><td>Curiosity</td><td>Persistence</td></tr>
<tr><td>Leadership</td><td>Kindness</td></tr>
<tr><td>Open-mindedness</td><td>Forgiveness</td></tr>
<tr><td>Honesty</td><td>Excitement</td></tr>
<tr><td>Bravery</td><td>Self-Regulation</td></tr>
<tr><td>Appreciation of beauty</td><td>Logic</td></tr>
<tr><td>Love of learning</td><td>Love</td></tr>
<tr><td>Humor</td><td>Fairness</td></tr>
<tr><td>Gratitude</td><td>Social Intelligence</td></tr>
<tr><td>Creativity</td><td>Prudence</td></tr>
<tr><td>Perspective</td><td>Modesty</td></tr>
<tr><td>Hope</td><td></td></tr>
</table>

Activity: Reflect on your values.

Using this chart will give you the opportunity to reflect on your values and the positive aspects of your life. Take a moment to engage in introspection and document your core values. It is crucial to identify and acknowledge your values as they not only serve as affirmations for your beliefs but also validate the instances in your life where you have embodied these values through your actions and experiences.

1. Self-Reflection

- **Description**: Consider what you value and what makes you feel fulfilled.
- **Examples**: Kindness, creativity, gratitude.
- **My Reflections:**

2. Feedback from Others

- **Description**: Ask for feedback on your strengths and contributions.
- **Examples**: "You're great at problem-solving," "You always go the extra mile."
- **My Reflections:**

3. Skills and Expertise

- **Description**: Assess your skills and knowledge in certain areas.
- **Examples**: Public speaking, software development, graphic design.
- **My Reflections:**

4. Achievements

- **Description:** Look at your past accomplishments and what you're proud of.
- **Examples:** Graduating from college, completing a marathon, winning an award.
- **My Reflections:**

5. Interpersonal Relationships

- **Description:** Consider how you contribute to your relationships with others.
- **Examples:** Being a good listener, showing empathy, making others feel valued.
- **My Reflections:**

6. Personal Traits

- **Description:** Identify personality traits that others appreciate about you.
- **Examples:** Patience, humor, dependability.
- **My Reflections:**

7. Passions and Hobbies

- **Description:** Explore what you enjoy doing outside of work.

- **Examples:** Painting, playing music, hiking.
- **My Reflections:**

8. Career Goals

- **Description:** Think about your long-term career goals and what you want to achieve.
- **Examples:** Becoming a manager, starting your own business, making a positive impact in your industry.
  - **My Reflections:**

Nurturing Social Connections

The significance of social connections in human life cannot be underestimated, as they are essential for various aspects of our development, reproduction, and survival. Across scientific disciplines, there is a consensus that humans are inherently social beings. Therefore, it is logical to assume that social factors play a significant role in shaping human health and overall well-being (Holt-Lunstad, 2022).

Cultivating social relationships and engaging in daily physical activity can profoundly influence mental health, including enhancing sleep quality. This underscores the interconnection between the chapters of this book in guiding you toward holistic well-being. To understand the combined effects of daily physical activity and social relationships on sleep disorder, a study conducted by Seol et al. (2021) examined a sample of 1339 community-dwelling older Japanese adults.

The participants were assessed for daily physical activity levels using the Physical Activity Scale for the Elderly and the extent of social relationships using the Lubben Social Network Scale. Sleep disorder was evaluated using the Pittsburgh Sleep Quality Index. The results of the study confirmed the positive association between physical activity, social relationships, and sleep quality among older adults. The findings of the study suggest that engaging in high levels of physical activity and having a wide range of social relationships are independently related to good sleep quality (Seol et al., 2021).

A study conducted with adolescents revealed that having supportive friendships and family relationships during adolescence can potentially decrease depressive symptoms in individuals who have experienced early life stress, such as childhood family adversity or relational bullying before the age of 11. Significantly, despite the negative impact of early life stress on subsequent social interactions, the study findings also suggest that positive social environments during adolescence can mitigate depressive symptoms later in life. Interventions that focus on fostering friendships and strengthening family support hold promising potential in reducing depressive symptoms among adolescents who have experienced early life adversity (van Harmelen et al., 2016).

As we explore the impact of friendships on subjective well-being, it becomes evident that positive interactions with friends form a crucial component of an individual's social capital. High-quality friendships, characterized by support, reciprocity, and intimacy, have the potential to significantly contribute to one's happiness and overall life satisfaction. Conversely, the absence of positive interactions or low-quality relationships may lead to feelings of anxiety and dissatisfaction (Amati et al., 2018).

Given the impact of social connections on an individual's well-being, it becomes imperative to understand the significance of creating and nurturing positive social relationships (Amati et al., 2018). In the following section, you can dedicate time to explore ways of improving social connections and building meaningful friendships to enhance overall mental and emotional health.

Improving Social Connections

Practicing active listening can help you deepen existing relationships. These skills are very important and yet they are not taught early in life. The practice of active listening involves fully concentrating on the speaker, trying to understand the message without judgment. Nodding and maintaining eye contact can help the speaker know you are engaged in the story. Practicing active listening can strengthen your social connections because people will feel valued, understood, and supported. As a result, they are likely to perceive you as a supportive individual who fosters positive emotions, which in turn enhances your reputation and builds strong, trusting friendships.

Social Connections: Self-reflection

Take some time for self-reflection and personal growth by engaging in this activity to improve the quality of your social interactions and friendships. Use the following questions as a template to guide your exploration. Write down your answers in a journal or notebook to keep track of your progress and insights.

- **Assessing Current Relationships:**
    - How would you describe the current quality of your social interactions and friendships?

Are there areas that you feel could be improved?

- **Defining Values in Friendships:**

  - What are the key values and qualities you seek in friendships? How do your current friendships align with these values?

- **Communication and Listening Skills:**

  - Reflect on your listening and communication skills. Are you actively engaged in conversations, or do you find yourself frequently distracted or waiting for your turn to speak?

- **Handling Disagreements and Conflicts:**

  - How do you handle disagreements or conflicts in your friendships? Are there healthy ways you can address differences and misunderstandings?

- **Initiating Social Interactions:**

  - Consider the frequency with which you initiate social interactions. Do you actively reach out to friends, or do you tend to wait for them to initiate contact?

- **Understanding and Supporting Your Friends:**

  - Do you try to understand and support your friends' interests and passions? How can you show genuine interest in their lives?

- **Expressing Gratitude and Appreciation:**

- How do you show appreciation and gratitude to your friends? Are there ways you can express your gratitude more often?

- **Overcoming Social Anxieties:**

  - Consider any social anxieties or fears that may be impacting your social interactions. How can you work on overcoming these challenges to foster more meaningful connections?

Note: Remember, personal growth is a journey, and this activity is designed to help you gain valuable insights and take intentional steps towards cultivating more fulfilling and meaningful social connections. Embrace this opportunity to enhance your social well-being and build lasting and supportive friendships.

Happiness

If happiness truly comes from within rather than from external sources, then it is crucial to nurture a sense of inner calm, peace, and motivation. People define happiness in many ways—like acquiring material possessions or achieving dreams—but these joys are often temporary. When the novelty of a new car, house, vacation, or job fades, so does the level of happiness they provide. Real, lasting fulfillment comes from cultivating an inner state of contentment that is not reliant on external circumstances.

Some days you wake up after a restful sleep, free of discomfort, and everything feels just right—your body feels great, the weather is perfect, your plans excite you, and life seems to flow effortlessly. On those days, happiness feels natural, and you wish every day could be the same. However, not all days go this way. Life, like nature, is ever-changing. You may have a restless night or face challenges at work, leading you to think, "I'm not happy today." Yet, true happiness is not dependent on external conditions, it comes from within and how you choose to perceive life's fluctuations.

These practices help you ride life's waves with grace, regardless of whether the day is sunny or stormy. Happiness is not in the perfection of the day, but in the choices you make to stay centered through it all.

When you feel good inside, with your body and mind in harmony, you will recognize that you are living a fulfilling life. You will smile at the sight of a simple wildflower, no longer rushing through your day or waiting for the weekend to bring relief. The healthy habits you have embraced will feel natural, and you may even wonder why you feel so light and vibrant, as though it is magic. But these habits are quietly working within you. By choosing to start this new journey, you are choosing to be healthy and happy.

The Help of Mental Health Counseling

While many strategies can support mental well-being, there are times when professional guidance can be especially beneficial. Mental health counseling provides individuals with a safe and supportive environment to explore thoughts, emotions, and life challenges. A trained therapist can help identify patterns of thinking, develop coping strategies, and provide tools for managing stress, anxiety, or other concerns.

Seeking counseling is not a sign of weakness. Rather, it reflects a commitment to personal growth and emotional health. For individuals experiencing persistent emotional distress or significant life challenges, professional support can play a valuable role in the journey toward improved mental well-being.

Takeaway

Cultivating mental well-being is a holistic journey that involves integrating various interconnected elements, from prioritizing restful sleep and adopting healthy nutrition to engaging in relaxation techniques and regular exercise. Each of these lifestyle factors works together to support emotional balance, resilience, and overall psychological health.

Mental well-being goes beyond the mere absence of illness; it plays a vital role in shaping overall health and quality of life. When mental well-being is nurtured, individuals are often better able to cope with challenges, maintain meaningful relationships, and approach life with greater clarity and purpose. Conversely, chronic stress and mental health conditions such as depression can affect physical health by influencing the body's immune response and increasing vulnerability to illness.

By intentionally practicing habits that support mental well-being, individuals can gradually strengthen their emotional resilience and cultivate a healthier mindset. Embracing practices such as gratitude, mindfulness, reflective journaling, goal-setting, and meaningful social interactions can help foster greater self-awareness and emotional stability. Over time, these practices contribute to a more positive outlook, improved coping abilities, and a stronger foundation for navigating life's challenges.

Prioritizing mental well-being is not a single action but an ongoing commitment to caring for both the mind and the body. Through consistent effort and self-reflection, individuals can develop the inner resources needed to maintain balance, foster personal growth, and build a fulfilling and meaningful life.

The Wellness Routine

174

The Wellness Routine

Based on the valuable insights presented in the previous chapters on the essential elements that contribute to overall well-being, I have designed this practical wellness routine to guide you on a transformative journey toward self-care and self-improvement. This routine is intended to help you incorporate healthy habits into your daily life while encouraging balance between your responsibilities and your personal well-being.

The purpose of this routine is not to create pressure or rigid expectations, but rather to provide a helpful framework that illustrates how the principles discussed throughout this book can be integrated into everyday life. These simple and foundational activities are organized according to key moments throughout the day. However, you can adapt them to your own schedule so that they align with your lifestyle, responsibilities, and personal needs.

Often, people begin a new exercise program or dietary plan with enthusiasm, only to find that after a few days other responsibilities begin to interfere. As daily obligations increase, these wellness goals may gradually fade into the background. The purpose of this wellness routine is to provide a realistic and achievable guide that can help you structure your day in a way that supports both your responsibilities and your self-care goals.

With consistency, many of these practices can gradually become part of your daily habits, allowing them to feel more natural and sustainable over time. Feel free to add additional healthy and enjoyable activities that resonate with you and contribute to your sense of well-being. You can also adjust the routine so that it reflects your unique lifestyle and priorities.

Some individuals find it helpful to set reminders or alarms on their phones to prompt them when it is time to engage in certain activities within their routine. Others may prefer to schedule these activities within their calendar or planner. The most important goal is to create a structure that allows you to balance your personal responsibilities with activities that nurture your physical and mental health.

Remember that this is a general wellness routine developed from the information and research discussed throughout this book. While these recommendations can provide helpful guidance, it is always advisable to consult healthcare professionals for personalized advice regarding sleep, nutrition, exercise, and mindfulness practices, particularly if you have specific health conditions or individual needs.

Wellness Routine

Morning

Wake up time:

— Gratitude

Upon waking, take a moment to observe your surroundings and gently bring your attention to the present moment. Cultivate a sense of gratitude by reflecting on something you appreciate in your life and thinking, "I am grateful for..."

— Positive Reminders

Repeat a few positive reminders or affirmations to yourself. You may choose to write them down in a notebook or simply say them silently or aloud.

— Mindful Moment

Spend a few minutes practicing deep breathing or mindfulness meditation to center yourself and set a positive tone for the day.

— Goal of the day

Start your day with a small, meaningful goal to accomplish. Setting an intention for the day can provide a sense of direction, motivation, and control over your daily activities.

— Morning sunlight

If possible and appropriate for your health, spend a few minutes outside or near natural light to help regulate your body's internal clock and promote alertness.

—   Journaling

Write down your strengths, qualities you admire about yourself, or personal accomplishments and past triumphs. This practice can help reinforce positive self-awareness.

—   Hydration Check

Drink a glass of water to help rehydrate your body after a night of sleep.

—   Nutritious Breakfast

Begin your day with a balanced breakfast.

Daytime

—   Movement Breaks

Incorporate movement breaks throughout the day to reduce sedentary behavior. Stretch, walk, or engage in a short activity to keep your body active and promote healthy circulation.

—   Stay Hydrated

Continue drinking water throughout the day to support hydration and overall bodily function.

—   Healthy Snack or Lunch

Choose nutrient-dense snacks such as fruits or yogurt, and aim for a balanced lunch that includes whole grains, lean protein, and a variety of vegetables.

—   Workout Time

Engage in exercise at a time that best fits your schedule. Whether it involves walking, strength training, yoga, or another activity you enjoy, track your progress and celebrate your achievements.

— Mindful Moments

Take brief pauses during the day to practice mindfulness. Bring your attention to the present moment by noticing your breathing, thoughts, or physical sensations.

— Social Moments

Create opportunities for meaningful social interactions with friends, family members, or colleagues. Positive social connections can add moments of joy and support throughout your day.

Evening

— Healthy Dinner

Prepare a wholesome dinner that includes lean protein, whole grains, and vegetables. Try to avoid very heavy or spicy meals close to bedtime. You may also enjoy experimenting with new healthy recipes.

— Plan and Prepare

Take a few minutes to organize the following day. Review your to-do list, plan important tasks, or prepare items you may need for the next morning.

— Relaxing Ritual

About an hour before bedtime, begin a calming routine. This may include activities such as reading, creating a relaxing home-spa environment, taking a warm bath or shower, or practicing gentle stretching.

— Limit Caffeine and Alcohol in the Evening

Reducing caffeine and alcohol intake later in the day may help support better sleep quality.

— Screen-Free Time

Try to avoid using electronic devices before bedtime. Reducing screen exposure can help your mind transition into a calmer state that supports restful sleep.

Bedtime

— Gratitude Reflection

Reflect on positive moments from your day. Ask yourself: What did I enjoy today? What am I grateful for in my life?

— Relaxation Moment

Practice relaxation techniques such as deep breathing or progressive muscle relaxation to help your body and mind transition into sleep.

— Sleep Sanctuary

Create a sleep-friendly environment by keeping your bedroom cool, dark, and quiet.

— Restful Sleep

Aim to enjoy approximately 7–8 hours of restorative sleep. Sweet dreams!

Note

Feel free to format and design the routine to suit your preferences and make it an engaging and interactive tool for self-care and wellness activities. The goal is to create a supportive guide that encourages consistent self-care and promotes overall wellness.

184

Conclusion

Congratulations on completing this guide to improve your overall well-being and mental health! Throughout this book, we have explored essential elements that contribute to your wellness, including quality sleep, nutritious eating, regular exercise, relaxation, and cultivating a healthy mindset. By incorporating these daily activities into your life, you can positively impact your physical and mental well-being.

As we discussed, prioritizing quality sleep is crucial for restoring and rejuvenating your body and mind. By implementing sleep hygiene tips and creating a tranquil sleep environment, you can optimize your sleep and lay a solid foundation for other wellness aspects.

Additionally, we explored the importance of nutritious eating and the role of a healthy gut in supporting your overall health. Mindful eating empowers you to make conscious choices about your food intake, while proper hydration enhances your physical performance and brain function.

Exercise is not just an optional activity; it is a vital priority that greatly impacts your physical and mental well-being. Finding the exercise that resonates with you and staying committed to physical activity can unlock the connection between your mind and body, allowing you to flourish.

Incorporating relaxation into your daily life is essential for counteracting the negative effects of chronic stress and cultivating inner peace. By embracing relaxation techniques and creating a calm environment at home, you can break the cycle of constant stress and experience the benefits of a rejuvenated mind and body.

Finally, we discussed the significance of mental well-being and how it impacts overall health and life quality. Cultivating a positive and robust mindset through practices like gratitude, mindfulness, journaling, and meaningful social interactions can enhance your mental well-being and foster resilience.

Remember, achieving true success goes beyond professional accomplishments; it involves finding balance and fulfillment in all aspects of your life. By prioritizing self-care, nurturing your well-being, and embracing a positive mindset, you can embark on a holistic journey towards a fulfilling and harmonious life.

As you continue on your path of personal growth and self-improvement, remember that progress is a journey, not a destination. Be kind to yourself, celebrate your successes, and be patient with any setbacks. Changing your habits might be uncomfortable at the beginning, but the positive effects make the change worth it. By consistently practicing the daily activities outlined in this guide, you can mentally detox from negative thoughts, develop positive perspectives, and live a more intentional and fulfilled life.

This wellness guide is your companion, supporting you through all stages of life. It is there for you during both the good and challenging times, reminding you to take a pause, breathe, and rejuvenate amidst life's responsibilities and sacrifices. Consider it your personal coach, guiding you towards a healthy and positive direction on your journey. In a world that often glorifies being busy, this guide serves as a gentle reminder to slow down, appreciate the present moment, and embrace the serenity and healing energy it offers.

The inspiration for this book comes from my meaningful interactions with individuals I had the privilege to work with, as well as from extensive exploration of research dedicated to improving human well-being. This book serves as a roadmap to help us move forward to a wonderful and fulfilling life. My hope is that the ideas shared in these pages nurture your resilience just as they have nurtured mine, empowering you to face life's journey with confidence, strength, and determination.

Thank you for investing your time in this journey of self-improvement and well-being. I encourage you to continue exploring, learning, and practicing the strategies that resonate most with you. By nurturing your well-being, you are taking proactive steps towards a happier, healthier, and more balanced life. Embrace these daily practices as valuable tools that support your growth, and remember that you have the power to create positive and lasting change in your life.

Here's to your continued growth, health, and well-being.

Bibliography

Abd El-Kader, S. M., & Al-Jiffri, O. H. (2020). Aerobic exercise affects sleep, psychological well-being and immune system parameters among subjects with chronic primary insomnia. *African health sciences, 20*(4), 1761–1769. https://doi.org/10.4314/ahs.v20i4.29

Amati, V., Meggiolaro, S., Rivellini, G., & Zaccarin, S. (2018). Social relations and life satisfaction: the role of friends. *Genus, 74*(1), 7. https://doi.org/10.1186/s41118-018-0032-z

American Psychological Association. (n.d.). Gratitude. In *APA dictionary of psychology*. Retrieved July 3, 2023, from https://dictionary.apa.org/gratitude?ref=based.inc

Athanasiou, N., Bogdanis, G. C., & Mastorakos, G. (2023). Endocrine responses of the stress system to different types of exercise. Reviews in endocrine & metabolic disorders, 24(2), 251–266. https://doi.org/10.1007/s11154-022-09758-1

Bauer, I., Hartkopf, J., Wikström, A. K., Schaal, N. K., Preissl, H., Derntl, B., & Schleger, F. (2021). Acute relaxation during pregnancy leads to a reduction in maternal electrodermal activity and self-reported stress levels. *BMC pregnancy and childbirth, 21*(1), 628. https://doi.org/10.1186/s12884-021-04099-4

Bhasin, M. K., Dusek, J. A., Chang, B. H., Joseph, M. G., Denninger, J. W., Fricchione, G. L., Benson, H., & Libermann, T. A. (2013). Relaxation response induces temporal transcriptome changes in energy metabolism, insulin secretion and inflammatory pathways. *PloS one*, *8*(5), e62817. https://doi.org/10.1371/journal.pone.0062817

Bray G. A. (2013). Energy and fructose from beverages sweetened with sugar or high-fructose corn syrup pose a health risk for some people. *Advances in nutrition (Bethesda, Md.)*, *4*(2), 220–225. https://doi.org/10.3945/an.112.002816

Bray, G. A., Nielsen, S. J., & Popkin, B. M. (2004). Consumption of high-fructose corn syrup in beverages may play a role in the epidemic of obesity. The American Journal of Clinical Nutrition, 79(4), 537-543. ISSN 0002-9165. https://doi.org/10.1093/ajcn/79.4.537.

Caputo A. (2015). The Relationship Between Gratitude and Loneliness: The Potential Benefits of Gratitude for Promoting Social Bonds. *Europe's journal of psychology*, *11*(2), 323–334. https://doi.org/10.5964/ejop.v11i2.826

Cena, H., & Calder, P. C. (2020). Defining a Healthy Diet: Evidence for The Role of Contemporary Dietary Patterns in Health and Disease. *Nutrients*, *12*(2), 334. https://doi.org/10.3390/nu12020334

Chauquet, S., Willis, E. F., Grice, L., Harley, S. B. R., Powell, J. E., Wray, N. R., Nguyen, Q., Ruitenberg, M. J., Shah, S., & Vukovic, J. (2024). Exercise rejuvenates microglia and reverses T cell accumulation in the aged female mouse brain. Aging Cell, 23(7). https://doi.org/10.1111/acel.14172

Choi, J. H., Lee, B., Lee, J. Y., Kim, C. H., Park, B., Kim, D. Y., Kim, H. J., & Park, D. Y. (2020). Relationship between Sleep Duration, Sun Exposure, and Serum 25-Hydroxyvitamin D Status: A Cross-sectional

Study. *Scientific reports, 10*(1), 4168. https://doi.org/10.1038/s41598-020-61061-8

Cloninger C. R. The science of well-being: an integrated approach to mental health and its disorders. *World Psychiatry, 5*(2), 71–76. (2006)

Cunha, L. F., Pellanda, L. C., & Reppold, C. T. (2019). Positive Psychology and Gratitude Interventions: A Randomized Clinical Trial. *Frontiers in psychology, 10*, 584. https://doi.org/10.3389/fpsyg.2019.00584

Di Liegro, C. M., Schiera, G., Proia, P., & Di Liegro, I. (2019). Physical Activity and Brain Health. *Genes, 10*(9), 720. https://doi.org/10.3390/genes10090720

Freeman, M., Ayers, C. K., Peterson, C., & Kansagara, D. (2019). Aromatherapy and Essential Oils: A Map of the Evidence. Washington, DC: Evidence Synthesis Program, Health Services Research and Development Service, Office of Research and Development, Department of Veterans Affairs. VA ESP Project #05-225. Retrieved from https://www.hsrd.research.va.gov/publications/esp/repo rts.cfm

Gamage, K. A. A., Dehideniya, D. M. S. C. P. K., & Ekanayake, S. Y. (2021). The Role of Personal Values in Learning Approaches and Student Achievements. *Behavioral sciences (Basel, Switzerland), 11*(7), 102. https://doi.org/10.3390/bs11070102

Get Enough Sleep. (2022, Nomeber 21). Retrieved from U.S Department of Health and Human Services: https://health.gov/myhealthfinder/healthy-living/mental-health-and-relationships/get-enough-sleep

Gillen JB, Percival ME, Skelly LE, Martin BJ, Tan RB, Tarnopolsky MA, et al. (2014) Three Minutes of All-Out Intermittent Exercise per Week Increases Skeletal Muscle Oxidative Capacity and Improves Cardiometabolic Health. PLoS ONE 9(11): e111489. https://doi.org/10.1371/journal.pone.0111489

Healthy Eating. (2021, February 17). Retrieved from Office of Women's Health: https://www.womenshealth.gov/healthy-eating

Herbert, C., Meixner, F., Wiebking, C., & Gilg, V. (2020). Regular Physical Activity, Short-Term Exercise, Mental Health, and Well-Being Among University Students: The Results of an Online and a Laboratory Study. *Frontiers in psychology, 11,* 509. https://doi.org/10.3389/fpsyg.2020.00509

Holt-Lunstad, J. (2022). Social connection as a public health issue: The evidence and a systemic framework for prioritizing the "social" in social determinants of health. Annual Review of Public Health, 43(1), 193-213. https://doi.org/10.1146/annurev-publhealth-052020-110732

Huang, Y., Li, L., Gan, Y., Wang, C., Jiang, H., Cao, S., & Lu, Z. (2020). Sedentary behaviors and risk of depression: A meta-analysis of prospective studies. Translational Psychiatry, 10, 26. https://doi.org/10.1038/s41398-020-0715-z

Järbrink-Sehgal, E., & Andreasson, A. (2020). The gut microbiota and mental health in adults. *Current opinion in neurobiology, 62,* 102–114. https://doi.org/10.1016/j.conb.2020.01.016

Kalia V, Knauft K (2020) Emotion regulation strategies modulate the effect of adverse childhood experiences on perceived chronic stress with implications for cognitive flexibility. PLoS ONE 15(6): e0235412. https://doi.org/10.1371/journal.pone.0235412

Karns CM, Moore WE III., and Mayr U. (2017). The Cultivation of Pure Altruism via Gratitude: A functional MRI study of change with gratitude practice. *Front. Hum. Neurosci.* 11:599. doi: 10.3389/fnhum.2017.00599 https://creativecommons.org/licenses/by/4.0/

Kudrnáčová M, Kudrnáč A (2023) Better sleep, better life? testing the role of sleep on quality of life. PLoS ONE 18(3): e0282085. https://doi.org/10.1371/journal.pone.0282085

Levinthal, D. J., & Strick, P. L. (2020). Multiple areas of the cerebral cortex influence the stomach. *Proceedings of the National Academy of Sciences, 117*(23), 13078–13083. https://doi.org/10.1073/pnas.2002737117

Lin, T. K., Zhong, L., & Santiago, J. L. (2017). Anti-Inflammatory and Skin Barrier Repair Effects of Topical Application of Some Plant Oils. *International journal of molecular sciences, 19*(1), 70. https://doi.org/10.3390/ijms19010070

Lindsay, E. K., & Creswell, J. D. (2014). Helping the self help others: Self-affirmation increases self-compassion and pro-social behaviors. *Frontiers in Psychology, 5,* 421. https://doi.org/10.3389/fpsyg.2014.00421

Liu, Y., Feng, Q., Tong, Y., & Guo, K. (2023). Effect of physical exercise on social adaptability of college students: Chain intermediary effect of social-emotional competency and self-esteem. Frontiers in psychology, 14, 1120925. https://doi.org/10.3389/fpsyg.2023.1120925

Ma, X., Yue, Z. Q., Gong, Z. Q., Zhang, H., Duan, N. Y., Shi, Y. T., Wei, G. X., & Li, Y. F. (2017). The Effect of Diaphragmatic Breathing on Attention, Negative Affect and Stress in Healthy Adults. *Frontiers in psychology*, *8*, 874. https://doi.org/10.3389/fpsyg.2017.00874

Muise, E. D., Gordon, R., & Ericson Woods, D. A. (2021). Ready, Set, Go! How the heart and lungs respond to exercise. *Frontiers for Young Minds*, *9*, 682141. https://doi.org/10.3389/frym.2021.682141

Nakamura, Y., Watanabe, H., Tanaka, A., Yasui, M., Nishihira, J., & Murayama, N. (2020). Effect of Increased Daily Water Intake and Hydration on Health in Japanese Adults. *Nutrients*, *12*(4), 1191. https://doi.org/10.3390/nu12041191

Naruse, S. M., & Moss, M. (2019). Effects of couples positive massage programme on well-being, perceived stress and coping, and relation satisfaction. Health Psychology and Behavioral Medicine, 7(1), 328-347. https://doi.org/10.1080/21642850.2019.1682586

National Heart, Lung, and Blood Institute. (2022, March 24). Sleep Deprivation and Deficiency. What Are Sleep Deprivation and Deficiency? Retrieved from https://www.nhlbi.nih.gov/health/sleep-deprivation#:~:text=Sleep%20deficiency%20is%20linked%20to,adults%2C%20teens%2C%20and%20children.

National Heart Lung and Blood Institute. (2011). Your Guide to Healthy Sleep (NIH Publication No. 11-5271). U.S. Department of Health and Human Services. URL: https://www.nhlbi.nih.gov/resources/your-guide-healthy-sleep

National Institutes of Health Office of Dietary Supplements. (n.d.). Vitamin and Mineral Supplement Fact Sheets. National Institutes of Health. Retrieved from https://ods.od.nih.gov/factsheets/list-VitaminsMinerals/

National Institute of Mental Health. (June 2021). Mindfulness for Your Health. U.S. Department of Health and Human Services, National Institutes of Health. Retrieved from https://newsinhealth.nih.gov/2021/06/mindfulness-your-health

Park, N., & Peterson, C. (2009). Character strengths: Research and practice. Journal of College and Character, 10(4) doi: 10.2202/1940-1639.1042

Pecora, F., Persico, F., Argentiero, A., Neglia, C., & Esposito, S. (2020). The Role of Micronutrients in

Sahli, H., Selmi, O., Zghibi, M., Hill, L., Rosemann, T., Knechtle, B., & Clemente, F. M. (2020). Effect of the Verbal Encouragement on Psychophysiological and Affective Responses during Small-Sided Games. International journal of environmental research and public health, 17(23), 8884. https://doi.org/10.3390/ijerph17238884

Stojanovic, M., Fries, S., & Grund, A. (2021). Self-Efficacy in Habit Building: How General and Habit-Specific Self-Efficacy Influence Behavioral Automatization and Motivational Interference. *Frontiers in psychology, 12*, 643753. https://doi.org/10.3389/fpsyg.2021.643753

Support of the Immune Response against Viral Infections. *Nutrients, 12*(10), 3198. https://doi.org/10.3390/nu12103198

Potera C. (2010). The artificial food dye blues. Environmental health perspectives, 118(10), A428. https://doi.org/10.1289/ehp.118-a428

Rajgopal T. (2010). Mental well-being at the workplace. *Indian journal of occupational and environmental medicine*, *14*(3), 63–65. https://doi.org/10.4103/0019-5278.75691

Ritchie ML, Romanuk TN (2012) A Meta-Analysis of Probiotic Efficacy for Gastrointestinal Diseases. PLoS ONE 7(4): e34938. https://doi.org/10.1371/journal.pone.0034938

Ritter, A., Franz, M., Miltner, W. H. R., & Weiss, T. (2019). How words impact on pain. *Brain and Behavior, 9*(9), e01377. https://doi.org/10.1002/brb3.1377

Schuch, F. B., & Vancampfort, D. (2021). Physical activity, exercise, and mental disorders: it is time to move on. *Trends in psychiatry and psychotherapy, 43*(3), 177–184. https://doi.org/10.47626/2237-6089-2021-0237

Seol, J., Lee, J., Nagata, K., Fujii, Y., Joho, K., Tateoka, K., Inoue, T., Liu, J., & Okura, T. (2021). Combined effect of daily physical activity and social relationships on sleep disorder among older adults: cross-sectional and longitudinal study based on data from the Kasama study. BMC geriatrics, 21(1), 623. https://doi.org/10.1186/s12877-021-02589-w

Smyth, J. M., Johnson, J. A., Auer, B. J., Lehman, E., Talamo, G., & Sciamanna, C. N. (2018). Online Positive Affect Journaling in the Improvement of Mental Distress and Well-Being in General Medical Patients With Elevated Anxiety Symptoms: A Preliminary Randomized Controlled Trial. *JMIR mental health*, 5(4), e11290.

https://doi.org/10.2196/11290   http://mental.jmir.org/
https://creativecommons.org/licenses/by/4.0/

Son, H. K., So, W. Y., & Kim, M. (2019). Effects of Aromatherapy Combined with Music Therapy on Anxiety, Stress, and Fundamental Nursing Skills in Nursing Students: A Randomized Controlled Trial. *International journal of environmental research and public health, 16*(21), 4185. https://doi.org/10.3390/ijerph16214185

Sun, D., Zhu, X., & Bao, Z. (2024). The relationship between physical activity and anxiety in college students: Exploring the mediating role of lifestyle habits and dietary nutrition. Frontiers in Psychology, 15. https://doi.org/10.3389/fpsyg.2024.1296154

Tee V, Kuan G, Kueh YC, Abdullah N, Sabran K, Tagiling N, et al. (2022) Development and validation of audio-based guided imagery and progressive muscle relaxation tools for functional bloating. PLoS ONE 17(9): e0268491. https://doi.org/10.1371/journal.pone.0268491

Uguccioni G, Pallanca O, Golmard J-L, Dodet P, Herlin B, Leu-Semenescu S, et al. (2013) Sleep-Related Declarative Memory Consolidation and Verbal Replay during Sleep Talking in Patients with REM Sleep Behavior Disorder. PLoS ONE 8(12): e83352. https://doi.org/10.1371/journal.pone.0083352

van Harmelen, A. L., Gibson, J. L., St Clair, M. C., Owens, M., Brodbeck, J., Dunn, V., Lewis, G., Croudace, T., Jones, P. B., Kievit, R. A., & Goodyer, I. M. (2016). Friendships and Family Support Reduce Subsequent Depressive Symptoms in At-Risk Adolescents. *PloS one, 11*(5), e0153715. https://doi.org/10.1371/journal.pone.0153715

van Kraaij, A. W. J., Schiavone, G., Lutin, E., Claes, S., & Van Hoof, C. (2020). Relationship Between Chronic Stress and Heart Rate Over Time Modulated by Gender in a Cohort of Office Workers: Cross-Sectional Study Using Wearable Technologies. Journal of Medical Internet Research, 22(9), e18253. doi: 10.2196/18253. PMID: 32902392. PMCID: 7511872.

Valdes, A. M., Walter, J., Segal, E., & Spector, T. D. (2018). Role of the gut microbiota in nutrition and health. BMJ, 361, k2179. doi:10.1136/bmj.k2179

Venn B. J. (2020). Macronutrients and Human Health for the 21st Century. *Nutrients*, *12*(8), 2363. https://doi.org/10.3390/nu12082363

About the Author

Anelys Perez is a mental health therapist and writer dedicated to helping individuals improve their overall well-being and lead more balanced lives. She holds a bachelor's degree in Psychology and a master's degree in Mental Health Counseling from Florida International University.

Through her work as a counselor, Anelys has supported many individuals in developing healthier habits, managing stress, and strengthening their emotional well-being. She has also worked with individuals recovering from traumatic experiences, helping them rebuild a sense of safety, resilience, and emotional balance. Her professional experience, combined with her personal interest in wellness and lifestyle balance, inspired her to write this book as a practical guide for those seeking to improve their quality of life.

Anelys believes that true well-being begins with recognizing one's inherent value and intentionally caring for both the mind and the body. Her approach emphasizes simple, sustainable practices such as mindfulness, healthy routines, self-reflection, and personal growth as essential elements for building a fulfilling and meaningful life.